MW00851002

A STUDY GUIDE TO
Calvin's *Institutes*

A STUDY GUIDE TO

Calvin's *Institutes*

by Douglas Wilson

canonpress
Moscow, Idaho

This book is dedicated to my colleague,
Dr. Roy Atwood, who was, if memory serves,
the first living Calvinist I had ever met. I knew
about them from history books, but here was one
who actually thought this way, alive in modern
times. Imagine my astonishment.

Published by Canon Press
P.O. Box 8729, Moscow, ID 83843
800.488.2034 | www.canonpress.com

Douglas Wilson, *A Study Guide to Calvin's Institutes*
Copyright © 2011 by Douglas Wilson

Quotations in this publication are taken from John Calvin, *Institutes of the Christian Religion*, ed. John T. O'Neill, trans. Ford Lewis Battles (London: SCM, 1961).

Cover design by Rachel Hoffmann.
Interior design by Laura Storm.

Printed in the United States of America.
All rights reserved. No part of this publication may be reproduced, stored in a retrieval system, or transmitted in any form by any means, electronic, mechanical, photocopy, recording, or otherwise, without prior permission of the author, except as provided by USA copyright law.

Library of Congress Cataloging-in-Publication Data

Wilson, Douglas, 1953-
  A study guide to Calvin's Institutes / by Douglas Wilson.
    p. cm.
  ISBN-13: 978-1-59128-086-6 (pbk.)
  ISBN-10: 1-59128-086-9 (pbk.)
  1. Calvin, Jean, 1509-1564. Institutio Christianae religionis. 2. Reformed Church--Doctrines. 3. Theology, Doctrinal. I. Title.
  BX9420.I653W55 2011
  230'.42--dc22
                                    2011007239

11 12 13 14 15 16   10 9 8 7 6 5 4 3 2 1

CONTENTS

Book Three · 133

The way in which we receive the grace of Christ;
what benefits come to us from it, and what effects follow

Book Four · 221

*The external means or aids by which God invites us
into the society of Christ and holds us therein*

INTRODUCTION

I became what is popularly known as a "Calvinist" sometime in 1988. It is a long and sordid tale, and to this day I am not *quite* sure what happened. There were various factors in play, as there always are with such things. The first was that I was preaching through Romans. I can recall telling one of our elders that I did not know what I was going to say when I got to "those chapters." When I began preaching through the book, I was not Calvinistic, and when I finished, I was. So that was one factor. I got to chapter eight and decided, "Oh, well," and just preached what it said. After all, I had nothing better to do.

Another significant factor was that I had encountered openness theology for the first time—the idea that chance governs some things, and God doesn't really know the future. The future does not exist in such a way as to *be* known. My conservative evangelical instincts recoiled from this, but because I was Arminian in all my "default" assumptions, I could not answer this position, given my premises. That was a problem.

The third factor was that I was entranced with the idea of "worldview thinking," applying the Scriptures to every aspect of life. This was an impulse that went way back, but it started to congeal in significant ways in the early eighties. With some other Christians, I was involved in the founding of Logos School, and one of our guiding principles had been to teach all subjects as parts of an integrated whole, with the Scriptures at the center. That's all very well, but when you go out there and try to find books by evangelical Christians on how the faith relates to politics, banking, foreign policy, agriculture, literature, economics, art, architecture, and medicine, you will quickly find yourself reading books by almost no one but Calvinists. I became aware of this, and decided that I would read Calvinists on anything except Calvinism. They were reliable guides all over the world—everywhere but their hometown.

But my inability to answer the openness position battered down my prejudices even at this point. I didn't like this "chance business," and surely, I thought, the Calvinists would have something good to say about chance. And so they did.

However, despite all this, I was still not prepared to ask Calvin into my heart. But that reminds me. If anyone who is not Calvinistic picks up this book for whatever reason, and his eyes happened to fall on the first sentence of this paragraph, and he is not amused, I would hasten to add that this was a joke, as in, not serious. That was another surprise. Calvinists, it turns out, have a very robust sense of humor. "Was that an example of it?" you ask. In reply I suggest that we just move on.

I was still not prepared for any of this to be true. There were two things going on. One was the argument itself and the other was my unwillingness to have the argument come to certain conclusions. I remember where I was standing in my living room when I told God I was willing for all of this to be true. "That's awfully big of you," the universe said in reply, and I thought I detected a note of sarcasm, but it was a big deal for me at the time. Up to that point I had *not* been willing for it to be true. Once I acknowledged that I would be willing in principle to lay down my prejudices, I did not immediately become a Calvinist. But I was no longer prevented from that happening by an intellectual dishonesty and pride. That surrender is why, when I got to that place in Romans, the fruit just fell off the branch.

To change the metaphor yet again, when I fell down the Reformation stairs, I hit my head on every step. I spent the first couple of years after all this happened denying I was "a Calvinist." This was because I had no intention of being a partisan follower of Calvin, regardless of how great he was. The church had had quite enough of the "I am of Paul, I am of Apollos" factionalism, and I did not want to add to it. The irony was I had learned all this Calvinism from Paul primarily—so I did not want to say I was "of Calvin." I did not want to do this because Paul had been very stern with people who had claimed they were "of Paul," and I wanted to follow him, not Calvin, because I was . . . of Paul.

And of course, by simply calling myself a "simple Christian," I should have realized that I was not necessarily avoiding the problem. There was a super-spiritual faction at Corinth as well, one that went well beyond allegiance to Paul and Apollos. You see, they were "of Christ," and it appears that they may well have been the worst of the lot (1 Cor. 1:12). There is an appropriate way to resolve everything in Christ (1 Cor. 3:22), and there is a hyperfactional way to do it. There is a sectarian way to be "of Paul," and there is a God-honoring way to do it (1 Cor. 4:14–16). But I did not know all this at the time, and so spent a goodly amount of energy denying that I was a Calvinist, when it was obvious to pretty much everybody that this was exactly what I was.

All I succeeded in doing was to make people believe that, in addition to adopting this appalling theology, I had decided to cover it all over with a layer of disingenuousness. It looked like I had taken the flinty rock of predestination and poured the oil of insincerity all over it. So finally I gave up, faced facts, and admitted that I was a Calvinist—but *only* as a form of theological shorthand. Jonathan Edwards put it this way—"I should not take it all amiss, to be called a Calvinist, for distinction's sake."[1] Aye, for distinction's sake.

Now I had read through Calvin's *Institutes* a few years before all this had happened to me. I was impressed at that time, but not convinced. I was simply doing my bit to become acquainted with the great literature of our civilization, which included Calvin, and, like I said, I was impressed. I was mostly impressed by the energy of his writing. This was real, whatever else it was.

Many years later, safely within the Calvinist fold, I was leading a men's forum for our church, and we began working our way through Calvin's *Institutes*. We would discuss a specified portion, and I had decided to draft study questions to help the men work through the material. Somewhere in Book 1, I think, we got waylaid and were somehow "overtooken by events," and so that project got set aside and slept peacefully for some years in my computer. But then, some years after that, the five-hundredth anniversary of Calvin's birth rolled around, and I noticed a number of Christian organizations gearing up to celebrate it. Princeton decided to publish a read-through-the-*Institutes*-in-a-year schedule on the web, and since I now had a blog, and a headstart well into Book 1, I thought I could use the year as a disciplined way of finishing this study guide. And, with a few glitches here and there, that is what happened.

Here are a few suggestions on the use of this study guide. C. S. Lewis points out, in his essay on the reading of old books, that classics are often unnecessarily intimidating for modern readers.[2] But many of them became classics precisely because they were so accessible—it is their

---

1. Jonathan Edwards, *The Freedom of the Will* (Lafayette: Sovereign Grace, 2001 [1754]), ix.
2. C. S. Lewis, "Introduction" in Athanasius, *On the Incarnation* (Yonkers: St. Vladimir's Seminary, 1996).

commentators that are opaque. As one old parishioner said to his pastor after the sermon, "This here Bible sheds a lot of light on them there commentaries." Calvin is engaging, pithy, funny, earthly, profound, and entirely dedicated to Jesus. So this study guide is not intended to get in between the reader and Calvin, but rather to provide a nudge that might get someone to pick up Calvin in order to read for himself. I would suggest reading the appropriate section in Calvin, then looking at the questions in the study guide, and writing down Calvin's answers in a separate notebook. The reader can then compare his answers with those that are provided in the guide. Given the scope of Calvin's work, it is not to be expected that every sound answer will be identical to another. My suggested answers should be considered more as discussion starters than as an answer "key." If you disagree with a suggested answer, it may be that I messed something up. It may be that you did. In either case, we can disagree with each other, which is something else that Calvinists do well.

Another possible use is for a leader to utilize this guide for a group study. He can assign a reading, give the questions to the participants beforehand, and then use the guide to help conduct the discussion. The same can be done for classroom use. This study guide is based on the Battles translation, but can probably be used with others.

In closing, be prepared for surprises in Calvin. He is a Calvinist, obviously, but he is no tidy, doctrinaire Calvinist. The words of Karl Barth are descriptive here—"Calvin is a cataract, a primeval forest, a demonic power, something directly down from the Himalayas, absolutely Chinese, strange, mythological; I lack completely the means, the suction cups, even to assimilate this phenomenon, not to speak of presenting it adequately."[3] To which I can only add, no kidding.

Douglas Wilson
Christ Church
Festival of the Anniversary of the Death of St. Dunstan's Cat, 2011

---

3. Karl Barth, *Revolutionary Theology in the Making*, trans. James D. Smart (Richmond: John Knox Press, 1964), 101.

INITIAL REMARKS

[1559]
John Calvin to the Reader

1. Did Calvin expect the first edition of the *Institutes* to be as successful as it was?
   No, he did not "in the least" expect that.

2. In what way did Calvin maintain that he had been maligned?
   He believed he had been maligned to the utter limit: "No one [has been] assailed, bitten, and wounded by more false accusations than I."

3. How did Calvin intend the *Institutes* to be ministerial preparation?
   To prepare men for the ministry by giving them easy access to the Word, and to enable them to advance in it without stumbling.

4. In what way were his commentaries linked to the *Institutes*?
   The Institutes *paved the way for his work in the commentaries.*

[1560]
Subject Matter of the Present Work

1. Why did Calvin translate the *Institutes* into French?
   It was in Latin to serve all men of learning, and he translated it into French desiring to bear fruit in that nation.

2. What value did Calvin place on this work?
   He did not want to seem to value it too highly, but he did think it opened up a way to a good and right understanding of Scripture.

3. The reading of the *Institutes* was meant to be an introduction to the study of what?
   It was an introduction to the study of the Bible.

4. How did Calvin want the reader of the *Institutes* to evaluate the teaching that was offered there?
   Calvin wanted the reader to compare what he was teaching to the teaching of Scripture.

PREFATORY ADDRESS
TO KING FRANCIS I OF FRANCE

[1]

Circumstances in Which the Book Was First Written

1. What was Calvin's intention in writing the first edition of the *Institutes?*
   To convey the rudiments of the faith to those who had a zeal for religion, that they might come to true godliness.

2. What made it necessary to expand the work so that it also became a defense to the king on behalf of the Protestants?
   The fury of certain wicked persons. Calvin thought their slanders made it necessary to kill two birds with one stone—instruct believers and present a confession of faith to the king.

3. If a mere accusation is all that is necessary to convict someone of wrong-doing, then what is necessarily threatened with extinction?
   No innocence remains for any man.

4. What was the central slander directed against the Protestants?
   That they were politically subversive and wanted to turn everything upside down.

5. If all the slanders were in fact true, what does Calvin allow to be just?
   That the doctrine and its authors were worthy of a thousand fires and crosses.

[2]

Plea for the Persecuted Evangelicals

1. What is Calvin's attitude toward France, his native land?
   He says he has as much natural affection as becomes him.

2. Since it was not the king's idea, the persecution of the Protestants was the result of tyranny from what kind of individual?
   It was more through the tyranny of certain Pharisees.

3. What, according to Calvin, constitutes true kingship?
   The recognition that one is a minister of God in governing His kingdom.

4. What were Calvin's adversaries unable to bear the thought of?
They cannot bear to admit weakness.

5. The persecutors insisted on maintaining at least one of two things. What were they?
To keep their rule intact and their bellies full.

[3]

Charges of Antagonists Refuted: Newness, Uncertainty, the Value of Miracles

1. How does Calvin respond to the charge that the teaching of the Protestants is a novelty?
He says that the teaching of God's word is no novelty.

2. If it is new, in what way is it new?
It is new to them.

3. In response to the charge that this teaching is uncertain or doubtful, how does Calvin turn the tables?
By pointing out that this is a pattern in Scripture (Is. 1:3), and by showing that they were not prepared to die for the things they claimed to be certain about.

4. In what way did miracles confirm the Protestant teaching? In what way not?
Miracles are the seal of the gospel. How could it be undermining miracles to preach the gospel? Contemporary miracles were unnecessary.

5. How did Calvin respond to the miracles that were purported to have established the teaching of Rome?
The same way Augustine answered the Donatists. The Bible warns of false teachers working miracles.

[4]

Misleading Claim That the Church Fathers Oppose the Reformation Teaching

1. If the contest between the forces of Reformation and those opposed to it was to be decided through an appeal to the church fathers alone, which way would it go?
The tide of victory—to put it very modestly—would be with the Reformers.

2. Were the church fathers without fault in what they taught? And what did the Roman church do with those faults? What illustration does Calvin use to portray this?

No, they were not without fault. But Calvin says the Roman church exalts the faults of the fathers and ignores the virtues. They gather dung amid gold.

3. Does Calvin sidestep the teaching of the fathers, or does he cite them to support his teaching?

He cites a number of them in support.

4. If the fathers were alive in Calvin's day, what is the last thing they would suppose the "sophists" of Rome were discussing?

The last thing they would suppose as the subject of discussion would be God. Their brawling arts were not theology, Calvin says.

[5]

The Appeal to "Custom" Against Truth

1. Why does Calvin not wish to be bound by custom?

To force him to submit to custom would be to treat him most unjustly.

2. What is the alternative to completely despairing of human affairs?

To grapple with the great evils or forcibly quell them.

3. What does the Lord do when many ages agree on a particular impiety?

Truth is not determined by majority vote. Scripture teaches what the end is for those who sin with the multitude.

[6]

Errors about the Nature of the Church

1. According to Calvin, upon what is the Church's existence based?

The reign of Christ at the right hand of the Father.

2. What are the two claims about the Church that Rome makes?

First, that the form of the Church is always apparent and observable, and secondly, this form is found in the Roman church and its hierarchy.

3. According to Calvin, does the existence of the Church depend upon a particular outward form?

No, it can exist under a number of forms.

4. What are the two marks of the Church that Calvin gives here?

The pure preaching of the word and the lawful administration of the sacraments.

5. To what effect does Calvin quote Hilary against the outward pretensions of Rome?

That the Antichrist would have all the splendor that some churchmen gloried in.

6. How does Calvin answer the argument for the Church from "pomp" and influence?

The synod that condemned Christ had pomp and influence.

[7]

Tumults Alleged to Result from Reformation Preaching

1. When the word of God is active, what is the response of Satan?

He takes up arms. He opposes no one when no one opposes him.

2. What did Satan try first to oppose the Reformation? What was his second move?

First he tried force. After that he tried disagreements and contentions, stirred up by the Catabaptists (Anabaptists).

3. What examples from Scripture does Calvin produce with regard to the same charge? List three.

Elijah was charged with troubling Israel, Jesus was accused of sedition, and the apostles were said to have stirred up the people.

4. In the New Testament, when the apostles saw that the gospel was resulting in tumults, what ought they to have done?

Calvin asks rhetorically if the apostles ought to have quit preaching when they saw the tumults that resulted. The answer, of course, is no.

[8]

Let the King Beware of Acting on False Charges: The Innocent Await Divine Vindication

1. How does Calvin address the charge that the Reformers were seditious?

He simply denies it, and he appeals to the common knowledge that the Protestants prayed for the prosperity of the king and his kingdom and were a common and simple people.

2. Even though they are on the run, what do the Protestants continue to pray for?

They continue to pray for the same, even though they are now fugitives.

3. What does Calvin believe should be done with those who "deck out" their vices in the liberty of God's grace?

He says there are laws that can be used to penalize such, according to their deserts.

4. If the king determines not to listen, how does Calvin warn him?
   He appeals to God as the ultimate judge, the one who delivers the poor from their affliction.

5. What is Calvin's final prayer for the king?
   That the Lord would establish His throne in righteousness and His dominion in equity.

BOOK ONE

THE KNOWLEDGE OF GOD
THE CREATOR

—————— CHAPTER ONE ——————

[1]

Knowledge of Self

1. In what sense can we say that Calvin's epistemology has dual starting points?

We begin with knowledge of God and with knowledge of ourselves.

2. Does Calvin argue for God's existence, or does he assume it?

He assumes it—he builds on that knowledge.

3. Would Calvin agree that in order to know God, a man must know himself as knowing?

Yes, knowledge of oneself would include this awareness.

4. Would Calvin agree that this means a man should start his epistemological journey by trying to come to a knowledge of himself?

No, he would not agree with that.

5. What is the motive a man should have in turning from knowledge of himself to knowing God?

If we know ourselves rightly, then we know how vain, impoverished, and infirm we are. This leads us to turn to God.

[2]

Knowledge of God

1. What does knowledge of God reveal to a man?

The fact of his own sinfulness.

2. What is the sole standard of all judgment of man?

The nature and character of God Himself.

3. Why is man easily satisfied with counterfeit righteousness?
Because we are inclined by nature to hypocrisy.

4. What is the relation between that which is "less vile" and that which is "most pure"?
Because of our hypocrisy, that which is a little less vile pleases us as though it were most pure.

5. What is Calvin's view of autonomous ethics?
It is not just unsupported; its judgments are radically skewed.

6. What will a vision of God do to our view of the study of philosophy?
What used to appear as glorious will become contemptible.

[3]
Fearing God

1. How does Scripture commonly represent saints who have felt the presence of God?
As stricken and overcome by dread and wonder.

2. What is necessary before a man rightly understands his own lowly state?
He must compare himself with God's majesty.

3. What powerful argument overwhelms men?
The kind of argument contained in the book of Job.

4. Although the knowledge of God and self are intertwined, what does right teaching require us to discuss first?
We must begin with God.

5. What can we do in our corporate worship to cultivate a right view of God?
We may confess together the things that Calvin mentions here— exalting the power, love, dominion, and majesty of God. We must keep the worship service God-centered.

—————— CHAPTER TWO ——————

[1]
Piety

1. What is a necessary prerequisite to knowledge of God?
Religion and piety are the prerequisites.

2. Would natural revelation be possible in an unfallen world?
Yes. There would have been a primal and simple knowledge of God had Adam remained upright.

3. Is it possible in our fallen condition?
   No, not apart from Christ the mediator.

4. What is the distinction Calvin makes between having right notions about God and "embracing the grace of reconciliation"?
   It is the twofold distinction between the Lord as Creator and Christ as Redeemer.

5. How does God reveal Himself in the universe?
   He created it, regulates it, and sustains it.

6. With regard to neutrality, what are the ramifications of Calvin's saying there is "no drop of wisdom and light which does not flow from God"?
   No good thing is possible apart from God, which means that, by definition, there is no neutrality.

7. What is the definition of piety?
   Reverence for God joined with love for Him, which knowledge of His benefits induces.

[2]

Trust and Reverence

1. What is the first thing a knowledge of God should bring to us?
   It should teach us fear and reverence.

2. The second thing?
   In the second place, it should teach us to credit Him with the giving of that gift to us.

3. What is a life that is not disposed to the service of God?
   It is a life wickedly corrupt.

4. Can any good be traced to a fountainhead other than God?
   None whatever. He is the source of every good.

5. Which God does piety worship?
   The one and only true God. It is impious to invent a god to worship.

6. Does piety shrink from acknowledging God's justice?
   Not at all. It reverences His justice, without shrinking back.

7. What is pure and real religion?
   Faith joined with an earnest fear of God, resulting in right worship.

8. What is the difference between a general veneration for God and true reverence?
   All men reverence God at some level. True reverence submits to His authority completely, especially in worship.

9. What is generally inconsistent with true sincerity of heart?
   Great ostentation in ceremonies.

CHAPTER THREE

[1]

Natural Knowledge

1. Does the human mind have a natural and innate knowledge of God?
   Yes, the knowledge of God has been implanted in us by natural instinct.

2. In Calvin's mind, is this up for dispute?
   No, he takes it as beyond controversy.

3. What effect does this knowledge have upon sinful men?
   It means that men who reject God are therefore condemned by their own testimony.

4. How is idolatry a testimony to this knowledge of God?
   It demonstrates that the idolator knows there is a God. Men do not willingly submit themselves to anyone, and that men are willing to bow down to wood and stone is a remarkable testimony to the depth of their conviction that there is a God.

[2]

Religious Invention

1. Have men crafted various religious superstitions in order to manipulate and control other men?
   Yes, they have crafted many things in religion—but this does not apply to true religion itself.

2. How can we say that this is not the origin of religion or piety itself?
   Calvin says that men would not have been able to manipulate superstitions unless man's mind had already been imbued with a firm conviction about God.

3. Does defiance of God make men bold?
   Not really. They may blaspheme mightily, but at the first sign of trouble they are most unsettled.

4. How does atheism testify to this knowledge of God?
   Atheism is at best intermittent. Knowledge of God cannot be consistently suppressed.

[3]
Religious Invention

1. Can men successfully eradicate the knowledge of God which is planted within them?
   No, it can "never be effaced."

2. How does "sardonic laughter" testify to the living God?
   It is the covering for the worm of conscience, gnawing away within.

3. What does Calvin mean when he refers to "degeneration from the law of our creation?"
   We were created to live our lives toward God, to live Godward. When we do not, we degenerate from this law of our creation.

4. Was this understood by pagan philosophers?
   Yes, Calvin argues, citing Plato and Gryllus.

5. What distinguishes man from beast?
   It is the worship of God alone that distinguishes man. Calvin is arguing that man is essentially homo adorans, *not* homo sapiens.

CHAPTER FOUR

[1]
Superstition

1. If men fall into superstition through ignorance, does this excuse them?
   No, not at all.

2. What is their blindness combined with?
   Their ignorance is mixed with vanity and obstinacy.

3. How do ignorant and superstitious men measure God?
   They measure Him by the yardstick of their own carnal stupidity.

4. What is the object of such men's worship?
   A figment or dream of their own heart.

5. What is the danger of wanting to know more than is fitting?
   It is joined with a false confidence.

[2]
Rebellion

1. How do men deliberately befuddle themselves?
   By extinguishing the light of nature.

2. Does Calvin believe that Psalm 14:1 and 53:1 are describing what might be called "pure" atheism? Is God's existence denied?

No. He believes they are denying His attributes and relegating Him to heaven.

3. Can someone deny God without formally denying His existence?

No. Whoever lives without fear of God is a functional atheist.

4. Can men through this rebellion get completely away from God?

No. God periodically brings them back to His judgment seat.

[3]

Idolatry

1. What is a common defense for superstition?

Men believe that any zeal for religion, however preposterous, is sufficient.

2. When men fashion an idol, what are they really worshiping?

They worship and adore their own ravings.

[4]

Hypocrisy

1. Can unbelievers fear God?

Yes, they can.

2. What kind of fear is it? What distinguishes it from righteous fear?

It is a slavish fear, forced by circumstance. Unlike righteous fear, it does not arise voluntarily.

3. What does the hypocrite want to seem to be doing?

He wants to seem to approach God.

4. What is the confidence of the hypocrite?

Ridiculous acts of expiation.

5. What does a hypocrite do in times of trouble?

He is impelled to perfunctory prayers.

CHAPTER FIVE

[1]

God Manifested

1. How clear is God's self-disclosure?
   Men cannot open their eyes without being compelled to see Him.

2. Does Calvin make a distinction between a seed of religion sown in men's minds and a revelation of Himself in creation?
   No, it is all a continuous part of God's self-revelatory continuity.

3. Can men look where God is not plainly visible?
   No. God is everywhere.

[2]

Divine Wisdom

1. Can anyone see God in creation?
   Yes. Educated men see more, but all men see plenty.

2. According to Calvin, what kind of study aids this?
   A liberal arts education reveals more of what God has done.

[3]

What Is Man?

1. What does Calvin mean when he refers to man as a microcosm?
   Man is a microcosm in that he is a rare example of God's power, goodness, and wisdom.

2. Why does the psalmist not hesitate to bring infants into the debate with atheists?
   Because nursing infants with their cries refute the madness of atheism.

3. Which pagan writer does Paul quote?
   Aratus, when he said that we were God's offspring.

[4]

The Revolt

1. What is the nature of the "detestable madness" Calvin refers to?
   That men deny God's existence after finding God in the excellence of man's own makeup—using that excellence as the reason.

2. How do men acknowledge they are fearfully and wonderfully made and still deny God?

By giving the credit to "nature."

3. How far does God's workmanship extend?

Down to the toenails.

4. How does Calvin deal with Epicurus?

By asking him to explain how a concourse of atoms can work together in the human body.

[5]

Confusion of Creator and Creature

1. Is the soul confined to the body?

No. The powers of the soul are not confined to the body.

2. What kind of example of this does Calvin give to make his point?

He uses the example of astronomy.

3. Can the universe be animated by a life force?

No. That is a weak and profane assumption.

4. According to Calvin, what is nature?

It is the order prescribed by God.

[6]

Grave Sin

1. What is the grave sin that can accompany an enjoyment of the Creator's gifts?

To receive those gifts without acknowledging the Giver of them.

[7]

The Kindness of God

1. Does God show kindness to all men?

Yes, in numberless ways.

2. In the natural world, are His clemency and severity both seen?

Yes, He shows clemency to the godly and severity to the wicked.

3. What should the punishment of one sin show us?

How much God hates all sins.

[8]
Theater

1. In what way is the world a theater?
   It is a dazzling theater, in which most of the spectators are blind.

[9]
How Hard Can It Be?

1. Is an understanding of God's existence difficult to come by?
   No. We can see it with our eyes and point at it with our fingers.

2. What kind of knowledge of God is worthless?
   The kind that flits in the brain.

[10]
The Point

1. What does knowledge of God lead us to?
   It arouses us to worship and leads us to the hope of a future life.

[11]
The Limits

1. In what way is evidence of God in creation worthless?
   Because of our sin, the testimonies contained there just flow away from us.

2. In what way are unbelieving men alike and in what way are they different?
   They are alike in the forsaking of God. They are different in that each one forges his own errors.

3. What is the problem with the whole tribe of philosophers?
   Their trouble is exactly the same.

[12]
Idol Factories

1. What flows naturally from the human mind?
   An immense crowd of gods.

2. When men invent things in religion, what happens?
   No end of superstitions.

[13]

Missing the Point

1. What do the princes of this world not understand?
   The wisdom of God.

[14]

Speaking in Vain

1. How does the manifestation of God in nature speak in vain?
   It illuminates the way, but cannot lead us in the way.

[15]

No Excuse

1. If the glory of God is declared through nature unsuccessfully, then
   why does this not leave us with an excuse?
   Because the fault or dullness lies in us.

2. Why can a man not claim to be deaf?
   *Because mute creatures declare God's glory, and eyeless creatures
   point it out.*

—————— CHAPTER SIX ——————

[1]

Actual Knowledge

1. What is the only source of actual knowledge of God?
   Scripture alone.

2. Natural revelation is sufficient to produce only what?
   Natural revelation simply involves the human race in the guilt.

3. What illustration does Calvin use to show what Scripture does?
   Scripture is like a pair of spectacles that enable us to see distinctly.

4. Is knowledge of God as Creator sufficient for a man?
   No, not at all. We must also know God as our Redeemer.

5. How can God be distinguished from the throng of feigned gods?
   *Scripture alone reveals the true God. The idols do not have that
   revelation.*

[2]

The Word of God

1. How has God rendered faith unambiguous forever?
   By making His revelation public.

2. What is necessary before a man can get the slightest taste of right and sound doctrine?
   He must be a pupil of Scripture.

[3]

Slippery Places

1. What is the source of our tendency to fashion new and artificial religions?
   The tendency of the human mind to fall into forgetfulness about God.

2. When we get away from the path of the word, what must we not do?
   Press on in the way we are going.

[4]

Additional Revelation

1. What is the role of special revelation over against natural revelation?
   To communicate to us what natural revelation cannot.

—————— CHAPTER SEVEN ——————

[1]

Church Authority

1. Where does the authority of Scripture arise?
   From God, and not from the Church.

2. What is a most pernicious error on this issue?
   That Scripture only has so much weight as is conceded by the Church.

3. Does the Church establish the canon?
   No. Calvin calls this sacrilege.

[2]

The Foundation of the Church

1. How does the Bible teach that scriptural authority precedes the authority of the Church?

By teaching that the foundation is the teaching of the apostles and prophets.

2. How does that argument go?

The Church receives the writings of the apostles and prophets but does not establish their certainty. They are self-authenticating.

[3]

What about Augustine?

1. What role does Church authority play in the mind of Augustine?

The authority of the Church is an introduction to faith in the gospel.

[4]

The Holy Spirit

1. What is the foundation for credibility in any doctrine?

The fact that God is speaking.

2. What is the secret testimony of the Spirit?

The same Spirit who spoke through the prophets must speak in our hearts.

3. Those who try to build faith in the Bible through disputation are doing what?

Wasting their time.

4. The testimony of the Spirit is superior to what?

It is more excellent than all reason.

[5]

Self-Authentication

1. Is it right to subject the Bible to proof and reasoning?

No, because Scripture is self-authenticating.

2. Does self-authentication mean from God's self or to our self?

It proceeds from God's majesty.

3. What is true faith?

That which the Spirit of God seals in our hearts.

4. What is the beginning of true doctrine?

A prompt eagerness to hear God's voice.

—————— CHAPTER EIGHT ——————

[1]

Superior Wisdom

1. Does human reason go the "whole distance" in giving us evidence that the Scriptures are God's word?
   No. If we have faith, human reason is helpful. But without faith, reason cannot reach that far.

2. Does this mean it proves nothing?
   No. It is helpful after the fact.

3. What is necessary before these secondary proofs are worth anything?
   Simple faith in God's word.

4. In the first line what does "this certainty" refer to?
   That Scripture is higher than all human wisdom.

5. There are three secondary helps listed, which are inadequate in themselves. What are they?
   Arguments, church authority, or other helps.

6. With the Spirit's work done, what role do they assume?
   They provide reassuring confirmation after the fact.

7. What is Calvin's first secondary argument?
   Other human writings, such as those from Demosthenes or Cicero, cannot affect us as powerfully.

[2]

Not Style

1. What is his second argument?
   Scripture is everywhere crammed with thoughts that men could not have originated.

2. Does the Holy Spirit reject all rusticity?
   No, He sometimes uses it.

3. Does He reject all eloquence?
   No, He sometimes uses it.

4. What brings the majesty?
   The Spirit causes majesty to suffuse the whole.

[3]

High Antiquity

1. What is his third argument?
   The antiquity of Scripture.

2. Ancient compared to what?
   All other writings, the Greek account of the Egyptians in particular.

[4]

Truthfulness

1. What is his fourth argument?
   The scriptural narrative tells the unvarnished history, showing the warts, as it were.

2. What are his examples?
   Jacob's "blessing" of Levi would be one.

3. What are some others?
   The murmuring of Aaron and Miriam would be one. Moses not preferring his sons would be another.

[5]

Miracles

1. What is his fifth argument?
   While miracles are not the absolute foundation, they do strengthen the authority of God's messengers.

[6]

Miracles II

1. How can this argument carry force for us when we have not seen the miracles?
   Moses had opponents in his day who would have objected loudly if there had been anything fishy about the miracles.

[7]

Fulfilled Prophecy

1. What is his seventh argument?
   Prophecies are fulfilled, contrary to all human expectation.

[8]

Fulfilled Prophecy II

1. What is his eighth argument?
   The incredible detail of some of the fulfilled prophecies.

[9]

Transmission

1. What is his ninth argument?
   The recognized antiquity of the writings.

[10]

Providential Protection

1. What is his tenth argument?
   The fact that God protected His word throughout the centuries.

2. What role do the Jews have in this?
   They are the "bookmen" of the Church, as Augustine calls them, preserving manuscripts they themselves do not use.

[11]

Simplicity

1. What is his eleventh argument?
   The Scriptures display a heavenly simplicity.

[12]

The Church

1. What is his twelfth argument?
   The Church has consistently given its testimony to the veracity of Scripture.

[13]

The Martyrs

1. What is his thirteenth argument?
   The faithfulness of the martyrs in testifying to the truth of Scripture.

CHAPTER NINE

[1]

Fanatical Appeal

1. Why do some abandon Scripture?
   They are caught up by a spiritual frenzy.

2. How can they justify this? What argument do they use?
   They say they are not following the letter which kills.

3. How does Calvin answer this from Paul?
   Paul had no less of the Spirit than these men claim, and yet he urged Timothy to give heed to the reading.

[2]

The Holy Spirit

1. Why do we need a distinguishing mark or test to tell if it is the work of the Holy Spirit?
   Because Satan appears as an angel of light.

2. Why is it not degrading to the Spirit to apply this test to Him?
   Because we are only comparing the Spirit's work to the Spirit's work. It is not degrading to marvel at His consistency.

[3]

Word and Spirit

1. What did Paul mean when commending the Spirit and condemning the letter?
   He was answering those who were calling people away from the benefits of the new covenant.

2. Can this problem still happen?
   Yes, certainly.

3. What does right reverence do in this situation?
   Right reverence defers to the word so that the Spirit might show forth His power.

4. How do Spirit and word work together?
   The Spirit testifies to the word.

5. When do these fanatics conceive these stupendous visions?
   They seize on whatever they have conceived while snoring.

CHAPTER TEN

[1]

The Creator God

1. What should it be enough for us to do?
   To recognize how God, the Maker of all things, governs all things.

[2]

The Attributes of God

1. What attributes are announced by God's name?
   His eternity and His self-existence.

2. What three things about God are necessary for us to know?
   Mercy, upon which salvation depends; judgment, which is daily directed against evil; and justice, by which believers are preserved.

[3]

Heathen Knowledge

1. How can we know that the heathen knew of the Most High God?
   Despite worshiping a swarm of gods, they all knew and spoke of the one true God.

2. What charge do we make against the heathen?
   That they were dragged into the worship of false inventions by their own vanity.

CHAPTER ELEVEN

[1]

Pictorial Representation

1. What does Scripture everywhere contrast God with?
   It contrasts the true God with idols.

2. What does the world pant after?
   The world pants after visible representations of God.

3. What corrupts the glory of God?
   Attaching any form to Him.

4. Why were the Greeks "not as bad" as the rest?
   At least they worshiped Him in human form.

[2]
God's Being

1. What did God make a point of telling the Hebrews about His appearances?
   That they saw no body.
2. What do representations of God do to Him?
   They sully God's majesty.

[3]
Direct Signs

1. Has God always "acted invisible"?
   No. From time to time He has manifested His presence.
2. Why does this not encourage the making of idols?
   They were all clearly symbols of His incomprehensible nature.
3. What did Juvenal know that the papists did not?
   That there is no visible likeness of God.
4. Is the temptation to idolatry limited to Jews?
   No, it is a common failing.

[4]
Images and Pictures

1. Why is silver and gold mentioned in Scripture along with clay and stone?
   So that the splendor of the materials might not accrue to the idols themselves.
2. How does Horace mock idolatry?
   In a way similar to Isaiah—he mocks a workman who is deciding whether a bit of a fig tree should become a stool or a god.
3. Is the prohibition of idolatry limited to graven images?
   No, it also excludes "likenesses."

[5]
Books of the Unlearned

1. Who first argued that images are books for the unlearned?
   Gregory.
2. What is the problem with this argument?
   God said not to do it.

3. What scriptural passages show this?
   Jeremiah 10:8 and Habakkuk 2:18. Images certainly teach, but they teach falsehood.

[6]
Contrary Opinions

1. Who among the early fathers differed with Gregory's view?
   Lactantius, Eusebius, and Augustine.
2. What early church council prohibited images in churches?
   The Council of Elvira.

[7]
The Wrong Images

1. What is the problem with many of the images made?
   They are examples of abandoned lust and obscenity.
2. In addition, why are there unlearned Christians around who need these "books"?
   Because the leaders of the church were mute when they should have been teaching.

[8]
The Font of Idolatry

1. Does Calvin agree that idolatry begins with memories of a hero?
   No. He says that this happens, but the origin of idolatry was more ancient than that practice.
2. What does he say the origin of this image-making is?
   Man's nature is a perpetual factory of idols.

[9]
Where Any Use Goes

1. Why does Calvin argue that worshiping follows looking?
   Because when men think they have seen God, they worship Him.
2. Why does the excuse that the one worshiped is limited to the image not work?
   Calvin says that whatever the pretext, this excuse does not work. Idolators have always distinguished the god worshiped from the image used.

[10]

In the Church

1. How do idolaters show their hypocrisy and inconsistency in how they behave?
   Why do they go on pilgrimage to see an idol just like the one at home?

[11]

Foolish Evasions

1. What is the "wily distinction"?
   A distinction between service and worship.

2. Why does it not work?
   Renaming a crime doesn't change it. Adultery is adultery, whatever you call it.

[12]

Art

1. Is Calvin opposed to art?
   No. Sculpture and painting are both gifts of God.

2. What may we paint?
   What we can see with our eyes. Therefore, we may not represent God.

[13]

The Pure Church

1. How long was the Church free from images?
   For about five hundred years.

2. What images belong in Church?
   Baptism and the Lord's Supper are the two assigned images.

[14]

Nicea

1. How does Calvin handle the scriptural arguments presented at the Second Nicean Council?
   He mocks them by simply repeating their absurd arguments.

[15]
Scripture Handling

1. How does Calvin handle their positive case for "adoration"?
   By simply pointing out how out of context their citations are.

[16]
Blasphemous Claims

1. What is the "pretense of antiquity"?
   It is the ancient defense of the use of images. But denunciations of the image worshipers show that there was ancient opposition also.

2. How did the idolaters overstate their case?
   For example, one John said that it would be better to admit all brothels into the city than to exclude images.

——————— CHAPTER TWELVE ———————

[1]
True Religion

1. What does the knowledge of God not consist of?
   It does not consist of cold speculation.

2. What does Calvin hold "religion" to mean?
   He opposes it to giddy license and says that piety confines itself within bounds.

3. What is the value of religion?
   It restrains men who would otherwise fly every which way.

4. Is it enough to concede just the supreme honors to God?
   No, because you can do that and still parcel out the various functions to lesser gods.

5. What does Calvin mean by the "vast throng" surrounding God?
   The lesser gods that all men, Jews included, have gathered under God in order to divide up the glory of His divinity.

[2]
Latria and Dulia

1. What is the difference between *latria* and *dulia*?
   It is a distinction without a difference.

2. Why was the distinction put forward by the Roman church?
   In order to justify the giving of divine honors to angels and to the dead.

3. What does Calvin think of the difference?
   He considers it an inept and entirely worthless distinction.

[3]

Honoring Images

1. Which (*latria* or *dulia*) did the Galatians offer those things which were not gods?
   They offered dulia, *and they were not therefore justified.*

2. In what realm is reverent kneeling before a creature permitted?
   In the civil realm, as a civil honor, it is permitted.

3. In what realm is reverent kneeling prohibited?
   In the realm of worship and divine honor.

4. Why is it prohibited?
   Because if we wish to worship one God, we may not pluck away even one particle of His honor.

——— CHAPTER THIRTEEN ———

[1]

God and Reason

1. What are two different kinds of errors that arise concerning God's spiritual and infinite essence?
   There are popular delusions and there are philosophical subtleties.

2. Why does God speak "sparingly" of His essence?
   In order to keep us sober.

3. How must we not measure God?
   By our own senses.

4. What does Calvin mean when he says that God "lisps" to us?
   He stoops to us in His condescension.

5. What does Calvin teach us in regard to the recent "openness-of-God" theology?
   Anyone of "slight intelligence" should understand that God speaks of Himself by accommodating knowledge of Him to our slight capacity.

[2]

Three "Persons"?

1. Why does God reveal Himself as triune?
   To distinguish Himself more clearly from idols.
2. What is the scriptural basis for using the term "hypostasis"?
   Hebrews 1:3.
3. Why does Calvin infer a differing hypostasis for the Son? On what textual basis?
   Because if the Son is the stamp of the Father's hypostasis, there must be a distinction. He argues from the verses immediately following Hebrews 1:3.
4. What is not lawful to make manifold?
   The essence of God.
5. How do translation issues bear on this?
   There are three hypostases in one God. Differences can arise about the words used to translate this, so long as agreement on the substance remains.

[3]

Terminology

1. Why do some object to such terminology?
   Because the terminology is not strictly scriptural, and some are squeamish about that.
2. How does Calvin answer this?
   He says it is wicked to disapprove of words that do nothing but explain what is in the Scriptures.
3. Does Calvin think the critics have a point at all?
   They could have a point, if they limited their objections to words that were not in Scripture and which detract from the simplicity of God's word. In that case, Calvin would embrace their sobriety.
4. How much should such terminology be used?
   Sparingly, modestly, and upon due occasion.

[4]

Screening False Teachers

1. When is such terminology particularly useful?
   In dealing with false teachers and accusers, who are very shifty.

2. What is the characteristic device of heretics?
   They cloak their errors with layers of verbiage.

[5]
The Limits

1. What is the fundamental affirmation about the Trinity which Calvin requires?
   That the Father, Son, and Spirit are one God, and yet the Son is not the Father, and the Spirit is not the Son.
2. Have the church fathers spoken on this with one voice?
   No, they sometimes use differing terminology.
3. What are the dangers of speaking about this at all?
   We are using limited human language to speak about an infinite God.
4. What is the essential attitude of the false teachers?
   They are tainted with a hidden poison.
5. Can someone scruple about trinitarian language without being a false teacher?
   Yes, so long as they are not doing so from arrogance or malicious craft.
6. What should these "squeamish men" be careful of?
   They should be careful not to be taken for evasive heretics.
7. Those who like to quarrel over words have what kind of problem?
   They nurse a secret poison.

[6]
The Thing Itself

1. What term does Calvin use for "person"?
   He uses the word "subsistence."
2. What distinguishes each from the other two?
   Each has an incommunicable quality.
3. How many subsistences are there?
   There are three.
4. Are there incommunicable attributes within the Godhead?
   Yes. Fatherness, Sonness, and Spiritness.
5. How are these different from what we normally speak of as incommunicable attributes?
   These are incommunicable, from God to man, but from one person in the Godhead to the other two.

[7]
The Deity of Christ

1. What cannot be imagined concerning God's word?
   That it is a fleeting and vanishing uttering, thrown out into the air.

2. Who or what impelled the ancient prophets to speak?
   The Holy Spirit, in the same way He impelled the apostles.

3. What is the Old Testament basis for the apostolic teaching that God created the world through the agency of the word?
   Moses tells us that in the creation, God spoke.

4. What are we to make of Calvin's use of Ecclesiasticus?
   He cites the passage, accepting it as true. But he does not call it Scripture, though he does accept it as the work of Solomon.

5. What is Calvin's understanding of Lady Wisdom in Proverbs 8?
   He interprets the figure Christologically.

6. What is the well-spring of all oracles?
   The word of God.

[8]
The Eternal Word

1. How do false teachers undermine the deity of Christ?
   They do it by "secretly filching away His eternity."

2. At what point do they think the word began?
   When God spoke for the first time.

3. What passage of Scripture does Calvin use to contradict this?
   He appeals to John 17:5.

[9]
Christ Our God in the Old Testament

1. What is the significance of Psalm 45?
   The eternal God is a throne for someone, and it cannot be a creature.

2. What is the significance of Isaiah 9?
   The Messiah is called God directly.

3. What is the significance of Jeremiah 23?
   The branch of David will be called Jehovah our Righteousness.

4. Who is Jehovah?
   Jesus is Jehovah.

5. What other passages are relevant to this question?
   Ezekiel 48:35 and Jeremiah 33:16.

[10]

The Angel of the Lord

1. Who is the angel of the Lord in the Old Testament?
   Jehovah.

2. Why is this described as a "foretaste"?
   Through the office of this angel, the office of Mediator began to be fulfilled.

3. Did any Old Testament saints see God face to face?
   Yes, in the person of this angel.

4. How was Christ in the wilderness with the Jews?
   In the figure of the rock.

5. Who shall come to the temple?
   The one to whom it belongs, that is, Christ.

[11]

Contextual Argumentation

1. What is Calvin's basic method of arguing for the deity of Christ from the New Testament?
   He takes a brief selection of passages rather than heaping up all of them.

2. What is the argument from Isaiah 8 and Romans 9?
   Isaiah says the Lord of hosts will be a stone of stumbling, and Paul says that prophecy was fulfilled in Christ.

3. What is the argument from John 12 and Isaiah 6?
   John argues that it was the glory of the Son that fulfilled Isaiah's vision.

4. Who is the true God in 1 John 5:20?
   Jesus is described there as the true God.

5. Who purchased the Church with His blood?
   God did.

[12]

The Divinity of Christ in His Works

1. What was the significance of Christ calling God His Father?
   Even the Jews of His day saw that He was making Himself equal with God.

2. In what way does Christ's governance of the universe demonstrate His divinity?
   Providential control of the universe is God's prerogative alone, and the writer of Hebrews ascribes this to Christ.

3. Did Christ possess a ministerial authority to forgive sins, or was it more than that?

More than that. He possessed the actual power to forgive sin directly, which only God can do.

[13]
Miracles

1. What is Calvin's argument from the miracles of Christ?

That His deity is demonstrated by the nature of His miraculous power.

2. What does he say about the fact that prophets and apostles also did miracles?

Even though they did miracles of a similar or greater magnitude, they were ministerial miracles, while Christ was showing forth His own power.

3. Is this response satisfying?

It is to me.

4. Would Calvin be willing to say that Christ did miracles because He was a miracle?

Yes. Christ is salvation itself. Christ is goodness and justice itself, and so forth. He is the miracle itself as well.

[14]
The Deity of the Spirit Shown through His Work

1. Does Calvin argue the same way with regard to the deity of the Spirit?

Yes, by going to the same source—Scripture.

2. To what does the universe owe its beauty?

To the Spirit's work upon formless matter.

3. Who is the active agent of God in all things?

The Spirit of God, everywhere diffused.

4. Does the Holy Spirit regenerate through His own power?

Yes, not by borrowing, but by His own energy.

5. What does the Spirit search, and what does this mean?

He searches the deep things of God, which can only be done by God. The Spirit is therefore God.

6. Who gives the faculty of speaking, according to Calvin?

The Holy Spirit.

7. How are the concepts *God* and *Spirit* used interchangeably?

By attributing divine power to the Spirit, Paul demonstrates the Spirit is God.

[15]

Express Testimonies

1. What is the significance of us being called the temple of the Holy Spirit?
   Because God is fulfilling a promise to make us the temple of God. He does this by His Spirit.

2. Who did Ananias lie to?
   He lied to the Spirit, and this is equated with him lying to God.

3. How do Paul and Isaiah agree in this matter?
   The Lord of hosts speaks in the Old Testament, and Paul says it is the Spirit of God speaking.

4. What argument for the deity of the Holy Spirit does Calvin reject?
   Equating the "spirit of the mouth" by which God created as the Spirit.

[16]

Oneness of the Trinity

1. What is the argument for the divine unity from Ephesians 4:5?
   That because faith is one, God is one.

2. Why is the baptismal formula important?
   It means that we are baptized into the name of the one God, who has shown Himself to be Father, Son, and Spirit.

3. Does Calvin believe it is appropriate to refer to the Trinity with a singular masculine pronoun?
   Yes. We are to look upon the one God, to unite with Him and cleave to Him.

[17]

Threeness in the Trinity

1. What is Calvin's term here for the Second Person of the Trinity?
   He uses the scriptural term of Word.

2. What is the point made by Gregory of Nazianzus?
   Calvin is delighted by Gregory's saying that he cannot think of the three without being drawn to the one, or of the one without being drawn to the three.

3. Why is it important to make distinctions within the Godhead, but not divisions?
   We make these distinctions because Scripture does, in the passages that Calvin cites. But these distinctions are "not a division," which would give us three gods.

4. Does Christ teach distinctions within the Godhead? Where?
   Christ does this in John 15:26.

[18]
Difference within the Godhead

1. Why must we be cautious in discussing this subject?
   Calvin wants to make sure he does not give occasion of "calumny to the malicious" or of "delusion to the ignorant."
2. What are the characteristics of each person within the Trinity?
   To the Father, we attribute the beginning of all things; to the Son, we attribute wisdom and counsel; and to the Spirit, we attribute power and efficacy.
3. What Scripture does Calvin use in defense of the *filioque*?
   He uses the description of the Spirit in Romans 8: sometimes as the Spirit of Christ and sometimes the Spirit of the one who raised Christ from the dead.

[19]
Relations within the Godhead

1. Is the Father the same person as the Son?
   No, He is not.
2. Does the distinct Father contain the Son?
   Yes. In each hypostasis the whole divine nature is understood, with the proviso that "to each belongs His own peculiar quality."
3. Does the distinct Son contain the Father?
   Again, yes.
4. What is the scriptural basis for this?
   John 14:10.
5. Again, what must our attitude be?
   One of humility. We must guard against "too subtly penetrating into the sublime mystery."

[20]
The Triune God

1. What does the name "God" signify, when there has been no particularization between the persons?
   It signifies all three persons, when no particularization is mentioned.

2. When there has been such particularization, what does the name "God" signify?

Then it refers to the Father.

3. What does Calvin mean when he says that the "name of God admits no relation"?

He means it is sacrilegious to compare the incomparable God in any way that brings God down.

4. Must the word "Lord" refer to the Mediator?

No. It would be foolish and childish to do so. The name "Lord" is sometimes used in Scripture for Jehovah.

[21]

The Right Spirit

1. Has the doctrine of the Trinity been historically troublesome?

Yes, in all ages.

2. What kind of spirit makes it so?

Satan stirs up ungodly spirits to harry orthodox teachers.

3. What demeanor is necessary in discussing the subject?

We must be sober and use great moderation.

4. What earthly example of our lack of understanding should keep us humble?

Our inability to figure out the nature of the sun's body, even though we can look at it daily.

5. Who is the only fit witness to the nature of God?

God is the only fit witness to the nature of God.

6. What does Calvin contrast with subtlety?

He opposes teachableness to subtlety.

7. What are we to be ruled by objectively?

We must submit ourselves to be ruled by the heavenly oracles, the Scriptures.

[22]

Servetus in the First Place

1. What motive lies behind trinitarian heresies?

A desire to overthrow the whole glory of God.

2. For Calvin, what is the *sine qua non* of orthodoxy?

That the essence of God is simple and undivided, belonging to Father, Son, and Spirit, and that by a peculiar characteristic, each person of the Trinity differs from the others.

3. What did Servetus hold concerning the persons of the Trinity?
   He held that the persons were "external ideas" which did not subsist in God's essence.

4. Did Servetus hold that Jesus Christ and the Holy Spirit were created?
   Sort of. He "indiscriminately mingles both the Son of God and the Spirit with created beings generally."

5. What did he believe concerning the spirits of believers?
   That the spirits of believers were coeternal and cosubstantial with God.

[23]
Other Rascals

1. According to other false teachers, where do Jesus Christ and the Holy Spirit "get" their deity?
   The Father infused deity into them.

2. What antithesis must we not admit?
   We must not admit an antithesis between Father and Son, as though the Father alone were God.

3. What is the argument from Romans 14:11?
   Every knee shall bow to God, that is, to Christ.

4. From Hebrews 1:10?
   That Christ is addressed as God.

5. From Hebrews 1:6?
   That the angels adore Christ as God.

6. Does the Son have His own being?
   Yes, the Son has being in Himself.

7. What is the significance of Romans 8:9?
   The Spirit is common to both the Father and the Son.

[24]
The Name of God

1. In Scripture, does the name God refer to the Father alone?
   No, not at all.

2. For Calvin, what is the argument for the divinity of Christ from Matthew 19:17?
   That Christ is not denying that He Himself is good when He says no one is good but God alone.

3. What is the argument from the need to worship Christ? What are the Scriptures for this?

If Christ is to be worshiped, then Christ is God. Calvin compares Philippians 2:10 with Exodus 20:3.

4. What settles the matter in Paul's writings?

Paul teaches that Christ was equal to God before taking the form of a servant (Phil. 2:6–7).

5. Is the Father the "deifier" of the Son?

No. To say so is a detestable invention.

[25]

The Essence of God

1. Is the essence of "Godness" shared by all three persons?

Yes. God is one in essence.

2. If the Father only is the essence of God, what does this do to the other two persons?

It would make the Father the deifier, making the Trinity nothing other than the "conjunction of the one God with two created things."

[26]

The Subordination of Christ

1. In what sense is the Son not subordinate to the Father?

He is not subordinate with regard to eternal essence.

2. If Christ never ceases to be the Son of God, then what follows from this?

It follows that under the name Father, the "unique essence of God" is "common to both."

[27–29]

The Early Fathers

1. Do Irenaeus and Tertullian support these false teachers?

No, not at all. These fathers are being misrepresented by heretics.

2. What does Justin teach?

Justin supports Calvin at every point.

3. What does Augustine teach?

Augustine is orthodox, and he is very careful to maintain continuity with the orthodox fathers before him.

4. What is the root problem in trinitarian errors?

An intemperate delight in speculation.

—— CHAPTER FOURTEEN ——

[1]

Creation of the World and Man

1. Should men try to "get behind" God's act of creation?
   No. We cannot and should not try.

2. Why did God give us an account of the creation?
   So that the Church might rest upon this and seek no other God than the true Creator God.

3. Why did God tell us how old the world is?
   So we could resist the monstrous fables found in Egypt and other places.

4. Any other reason?
   So that God's eternity might shine forth clearly.

5. How old does Calvin believe the world to be?
   About six thousand years old.

6. Should we ask why God waited so long? Why not?
   No. Human reason would fail a hundred times on the way to that solution.

7. What was Augustine's great *bon mot?*
   When asked what God was doing before the creation, Augustine replied that He had been building hell for the curious.

8. Were spectacles invented in Calvin's day?
   Apparently. He refers to them.

9. Is there any cause higher than God's will? What happens if we attribute one?
   No, there is not. We do wrong to God if we attribute a higher cause.

10. Do we have enough to study within the created order?
    Yes. Why speculate beyond what is given, when we have so much to study within the created order?

[2]

Six Days

1. Did God create the world in a moment?
   No, creation was not instantaneous.

2. How long did it take?
   God created over the course of six days.

3. What does the Sabbath invite us to do?
   It invites us to the cultivation of quiet.

4. For Calvin, was the Trinity involved in the six-day creation?
Yes. The creation was brought into being by the triune God.

[3]
Creation of the World and Man

1. Why does Calvin say the creation of the angels is not mentioned?
Moses accommodated himself to the rudeness of the common folk, mentioning only the creation of those things which everybody sees.

2. Why was divinity sometimes attributed to angels?
Because of the preeminence of the angelic nature, many have thought them wronged if they are not given divine honors.

3. What would Manichean dualism do, according to Calvin?
Rob God of the glory of creation.

4. How has Manichean thinking resurfaced in our contemporary evangelical thinking?
It has resurfaced whenever sovereignty is accorded to the devil, asserting that he can do certain things "against God's will and resistance."

5. Where does sin come from, according to Calvin? Where does it *not* come from?
It arises from a corruption of nature. It does not arise from nature itself.

6. Why does the Nicene Creed mention the creation of invisible things?
To makes sure we attribute God's sovereignty beyond what our eyes can see.

[4]
Vain Discussion of Angels

1. What is our one rule in discussions of angels, according to Calvin?
That we should avoid speculation. Always maintain "modesty and sobriety."

2. What is the *content* of such empty speculations?
The "nature, orders, and number of angels," speculated on apart from Scripture.

3. What does the fellow called Dionysus contribute to our knowledge of angels?
For the most part, he contributes "nothing but talk."

4. What is a theologian's task?
It is to strengthen consciences, not to divert ears with chatter.

[5]

Scriptural Discussion of Angels

1. What is the name for angels in Luke 2:13? Why?
   They are called hosts. They bear a soldier's task, as bodyguards surround a prince.

2. What is another name for them in Ephesians 1:21?
   They are called virtues there.

3. In Colossians 1:16?
   Paul calls them thrones.

4. Is it proper, ever, to call them gods?
   Yes. More than once Scripture does so.

5. Does Calvin agree with the common understanding that the angel of the Lord frequently refers to Christ?
   Yes, he agrees.

6. How does Calvin defend calling angels "gods"?
   If the term can be applied to men sometimes, then how much more is it appropriate to apply it to angels?

[6–7]

Guardian Angels

1. How does guardianship apply first?
   It applies in the first place to Christ.

2. What is the second level of reference?
   In the second place, it applies to all believers.

3. What are the Scriptures for this?
   There are many, but Psalm 90:11 and Psalm 34:7 are among them.

4. Does Calvin think individual Christians have an individual guardian?
   He dares not affirm that with any confidence.

5. What does he think about angels generally guarding believers generally?
   He affirms that the angels collectively watch over our salvation.

6. And what is his view of a good and bad angel, perched on each shoulder?
   He says, in effect, that it is none of our business.

[8]

More about Angels

1. What does Calvin think about sketching detailed hierarchies for the angels? Why?
   Because he is reluctant to go beyond what is written, he doesn't have much to say.

2. How many angels are there?
   Scripture teaches that there are "many."

3. What sort of body do angels have?
   They lack bodily form but are represented under different figures for the sake of our better comprehension.

4. What must we be careful not to do in discussing this subject?
   We must not "probe too curiously' or "talk too confidently."

[9]

Angels as Real Creatures

1. Does Calvin believe angels to be real?
   They are not mere ideas, but have actual existence.

2. Do angels have features of personality?
   Yes. For example, joy is attributed to them (Lk. 15:10).

[10]

Angels Not Divine

1. Once we have settled that angels exist, what is the opposite error that we can fall into?
   We can make the mistake of attributing divine glory to them.

2. What does this error do to the glory that is due to Christ?
   Christ's glory is obscured.

[11]

Angels as Ministers

1. What task do the angels have?
   Among other things, to provide for the safety of believers.

2. What example of this does Calvin give?
   He gives the example of Elisha's servant (2 Kgs. 6:17).

[12]

Angels Not to Be a Distraction

1. If angels are given to help us stay close to God, what "preposterous" error might we commit?
   It is preposterous to allow angels to lead us away from God.
2. Does God promise us angelic help so that we may "divide our trust"?
   No, not at all.

[13]

Scripture Equips Us against the Devil

1. Why does Scripture describe the devil in terms of great power?
   To make us more cautious and watchful.
2. How does this help us?
   We have been forewarned against the threats we face.

[14]

The Realm of Wickedness

1. Why should we not yield to idleness?
   Because we are at war with a great host.
2. How great are the forces against us?
   It is an empire of wickedness.

[15]

The Ongoing War

1. What is the status of our relationship to the devil?
   We are engaged in an "irreconcilable war with him."
2. What does Calvin mean by "consummate depravity"?
   That disposition dedicated to attacking God's glory and man's salvation.

[16]

The Devil Originally Good

1. Was the devil created malicious?
   No. His malice came from his perversion, not from his creation.
2. How does Christ hint that the devil was once in the truth?
   Christ said that he "abode not in the truth."

3. On what subject must we not feed our curiosity?
We must not feed them on "empty histories."

[17]

The Devil under God

1. How many of the devil's actions does God control?
Absolutely all of them.

2. What are three passages cited by Calvin to show the devil answers to God?
1 Kings 22:20–22; 1 Samuel 16:14; and Psalm 78:49.

3. Does the devil want to obey his Creator?
Not at all, but he cannot overthrow God's sovereignty over him.

[18]

Victory

1. What impact do the devils have on believers?
They can do everything but "vanquish or crush" them.

2. On unbelievers?
These they "subdue and drag away."

3. Can believers ever be utterly thrown down by the devil?
No, never.

4. What is the nature of the reciprocity between Christ's kingdom and the devil's?
To the extent that Christ's kingdom is built up, to that extent Satan's kingdom falls.

[19]

Devils Are Real

1. What do angels and devils have in common?
They are both real. They are not thoughts, but actualities.

2. How does eternal punishment teach us about the reality of angels?
Eternal fire would not have been prepared for nonexistent entities.

[20]

Fruitful Creation

1. Is Calvin insensible to the beauties of the creation?
No. He says we should not be ashamed to take "pious delight" in the works of God.

2. What image does he use to describe it?
   He calls it "this most beautiful theater."
3. Is the beauty of nature the chief evidence of faith?
   No, but it is the first evidence in the order of nature.
4. Does Calvin believe God created *ex nihilo?*
   Yes. God by the power of His word and Spirit created "heaven and earth out of nothing."

[21]

Seeing God's Works

1. How much time could we spend in contemplating God's wisdom in the creation, "as in mirrors"?
   We could be unceasingly occupied with it.
2. Why does Calvin have to bring his discussion of this to an end?
   Otherwise, there would be no end to it.

[22]

Contemplating Creational Goodness

1. What should our response be to all of this?
   Our response should be one of thankfulness and trust.

2. What is the actual apparent difficulty in six-day creation?
   The question is why it took so long.

—— CHAPTER FIFTEEN ——

[1]

The Image of God

1. To what truth about knowledge does Calvin return in this section?
   He repeats how he began the Institutes. *We cannot know God without knowing ourselves and vice versa.*

2. What two aspects of himself must man know in order to know God rightly?
   We must know how we were before the Fall, and we must know what our condition became after the Fall.

3. What happens if men blame their failings on nature?
   It has the effect of blaming God.

[2]
Division of Body and Soul

1. What does Calvin understand the word soul to mean?
As an "immortal yet created" essence.

2. What is the "undoubted sign of the immortal spirit"?
The conscience.

3. In what ways does sleep indicate the immortality of the spirit?
It suggests things that never happened and presentiments of the future.

[3]
The Seat of God's Image

1. According to Calvin, is the image of God in man primarily spiritual or physical?
He says the proper seat of God's image is the soul.

2. What argument of Osiander's does Calvin consider and reject?
The idea that Christ would have become man even if Adam had not fallen.

[4]
Renewal through Christ

1. Since the image of God in man is a desolate ruin, how can we tell what it is like?
By looking to Christ, the second Adam.

2. Do the elect in this life reflect any more of that image?
Yes, as we are renewed in knowledge, righteousness, and holiness.

3. When does it attain its full splendor?
In heaven, in the resurrection.

4. What does Calvin think of Augustine's view that the soul reflects the Trinity?
He says that it is "by no means sound."

[5]
A Manichean Error

1. Who reintroduced the Manichean error?
That scamp Servetus.

2. What does Calvin think of the idea that the soul was formed *ex Deo* instead of created *ex nihilo*?
He rejects it, saying that this would make God as mutable as man.

[6]

The Soul and Its Faculties

1. Which of the philosophers, according to Calvin, had a decent conception of the soul?
   He says that Plato did okay.

2. The more someone approaches God, the more he proves what?
   The more he proves himself endowed with reason.

[7]

Understanding and Will

1. According to Calvin, what are the two faculties of the soul?
   Understanding and will.

2. And which of these two is the governor?
   Calvin says that understanding is the "leader and governor."

[8]

Adam's Freedom

1. Prior to the Fall, did Adam have the resources to attain to eternal life?
   Yes. He, by free will, had the power, if he chose, to attain to eternal life.

2. Why should we not invoke the doctrine of secret predestination in this discussion?
   Because we are not talking about what could or could not happen, but rather discussing "what man's nature was like."

3. Why do the "philosophers" misunderstand the nature of man?
   They are looking for a building in the midst of a ruin.

—————— CHAPTER SIXTEEN ——————

[1]

Creation and Providence

1. Why can the doctrines of creation and providence not be separated?
   Because we do not stop where carnal sense stops, with the fact of creation and potential energy within it. We see that faith must "penetrate more deeply."

2. Would God make something as majestic as the universe without caring for it afterwards?
No. What He created, He also "sustains, nourishes, and cares for."

[2]
No Such Thing as Chance

1. How does Calvin describe the opinion that chance governs?
He calls it a "depraved opinion."

2. What governs all things?
All things are governed by God's secret plan.

[3]
God's Providence

1. Is God's providence general or specific and detailed?
God's sovereignty extends into "individual and particular motions."

2. How does Calvin deal with the claims of astrology?
By pointing out that behind any motions in the stars we find that all things are governed by "God's secret plan."

[4]
The Nature of Providence

1. What does the word providence *not* refer to?
It does not mean that God watches idly from heaven.

2. Is providence limited to foreknowledge?
No, it means more than "bare foreknowledge."

3. If God governs the laws of nature only, what has been taken from Him?
They take away His determination, while trying to leave His might. They take away the "chief thing."

[5]
God's Special Providence

1. If God controls the general laws only, what is no place left for?
No place is left for "God's work" in particular events.

2. If singular prosperity for the crops one year is from God, then what does that mean for "scarcity and famine"?
Scarcity and famine are His curse and vengeance.

3. If fields are struck with hail and storms, what is this a sign of?
It is a sign of His certain and special vengeance.

[6]

God's Providence and Men

1. What "absurd folly" do "miserable men" take upon themselves?
   Acting apart from God, when they cannot even speak apart from Him.

2. What one thing that might be thought of as governed by chance is actually governed by God?
   The casting of lots, though even that is attributed to God in Scripture.

[7]

Natural Occurrences

1. What kind of testimonies are particular events?
   They are testimonies of God's singular providence.

2. What passage does Calvin cite to show God controls all winds?
   Exodus 16:13.

3. The waves?
   Psalm 107:25.

4. The opening and closing of wombs?
   Psalm 127:3.

5. The nourishment that bread gives?
   Isaiah 3:1.

[8]

Not Fate or Fortune

1. Why does Calvin not believe in fate?
   The apostle Paul teaches us to avoid that profane novelty (1 Tim. 6:20).

2. What does the necessity of the future not rest on?
   It does not rest upon fortune or chance.

3. And what is it based on?
   It must be wholly referred to divine providence.

[9]

From Another Vantage

1. Though God controls all events, what does it look like from our perspective?
   To us, they seem fortuitous.

2. Is it lawful to speak of these events from our perspective?
   Certainly, we may speak as we see from our vantage.

3. And what must we remember at the same time?
We must remember that God is behind all of it.

─────── CHAPTER SEVENTEEN ───────

[1]

The Meaning of God's Ways

1. What are the three things that must be remembered with regard to God's providence?
It applies to the future as well as the past; it can work with or without an intermediary; and it reveals God's concern for the whole human race and especially for the Church.

2. What temptation occurs to us as we see God's control over all events?
The idea creeps in that God makes sport of men by throwing them around like balls.

3. Do hard providences glorify God? What scriptural passage does Calvin use to make this point?
Yes, they do, provided our eyes are pure. Calvin cites John 9:3.

[2]

Respect God's Ways

1. How does Calvin describe those who do not submit to this doctrine with fear and reverence?
As barking and biting dogs.

2. And what causes their problem?
They do not wish anything to be lawful for God other than "what their own reason prescribes for themselves."

3. What verse from Moses sums up Calvin's approach?
Deuteronomy 29:29. The secret things belong to God, and the revealed things belong to us and to our children.

[3]

Man's Responsibility

1. Give several examples of pagan responses to the gods' disposition of human affairs.
Homer's Agamemnon blames Zeus and fate both. A youth in Plautus says that the fates drive men.

2. How does this view lead to an excusing of sin?
A belief in fate allows for infinite rationalizations. And all men do this to "attain what they desired."

[4]

Due Prudence

1. Should the fact that God's providential care extends to all things prevent us from exercising due prudence?
Not at all. We should look to our affairs but in submission to His will.

2. If God offers secondary helps and instruments, should we use them?
Yes—"if He offers helps," we should "use them."

3. Does God ordain the means as well as the ends?
Yes. God determines all things, means and ends both.

4. Does God's providence come to us "naked"?
No. God clothes it with the means employed.

[5]

No Excuses

1. What do wicked men want to do with the doctrine of providence?
They want to accuse God on the basis of it, making Him the author of evil.

2. Does Calvin agree that they are serving God's will through the sins they commit?
No, he denies it.

3. Does he agree that if God had not willed it, it would not be done?
Yes, he agrees with that.

4. What are the two things they must do in order to justify their sin, and which they cannot do?
They must either involve God in their iniquity, or they must cloak their own sin with His justice, and they can do neither.

[6]

True Solace

1. According to Calvin, should believers take comfort from God being the principal cause of all things, while at the same time giving attention to secondary causes in their proper place?
Yes, they should.

2. What is the principal purpose of biblical history?
It is to show that God watches over His saints.

[7]
When God Blesses

1. Can God turn the activity of our enemies to our good?
   Yes, as the example of Israel with the Egyptians shows.
2. What is the only thing that can make all things prosper?
   It is by the Lord's blessing alone that all things prosper.

[8]
Certainty about Prosperity

1. Why was Joseph able to forget the injustice committed by his brothers?
   Because he knew that the Lord was in it.
2. What was Job's most beautiful thought?
   That the Lord had given, the Lord had taken away, and blessed be the name of the Lord.
3. What do we learn when we "mount up to God" when others treat us wickedly?
   That the whole thing was permitted and sent "by God's just dispensation."

[9]
No Contempt for Ordinary Causes

1. What is a godly man's attitude toward secondary causes?
   He will not overlook them.
2. Will such a man consider his errors less serious or culpable?
   He will by no means consider his own misdeeds less serious.

[10]
Life without Such Certainty

1. Where might we encounter potential harm?
   No matter where we go, there is potential harm.
2. If this were governed by fortune alone, what would our attitude have to be?
   We would be tied up with perpetual anxiety, with a sword "hanging over [our] neck."

[11]

Joyful Trust

1. If we would rightly dread fortune, what may our attitude toward God's providence be?
   We should fearlessly commit ourselves to God.

2. Can anything happen that God does not determine?
   Nothing.

3. When the world appears to be "aimlessly tumbled about," what is the Lord doing?
   The Lord is everywhere at work.

[12]

Objections

1. What is an obvious objection to this position?
   That the Bible sometimes speaks of God changing mid-course.

2. Name three places cited by Calvin where Scripture mentions God "repenting."
   Genesis 6:6; 1 Samuel 15:11; and Jeremiah 18:8.

3. Why does Calvin take the citation about God repenting that He had made Saul king figuratively?
   Because in the same passage God is described as not being like a man, that He should repent.

[13]

God Accommodates Our Frailty

1. What problem is God solving when He speaks figuratively in this way?
   God is adjusting Himself to our capacity for understanding.

2. In such passages, what should we understand by the word "repenting"?
   We ought to understand nothing other than a "change of action."

[14]

God Executes His Plan

1. How does the context of God's warnings to Nineveh and Hezekiah help us understand their underlying meaning?
   God uses His threats in order to bring about a change in us.

———— CHAPTER EIGHTEEN ————

[1]
Not Just Bare Permission

1. Concerning God's providence, what is the "more difficult question"?
   *The more difficult question is the matter of God controlling evil.
   How can He control it without being defiled by it?*

2. Does Calvin allow the distinction between doing and permitting?
   No, he does not.

3. Why would we describe Calvin as a strict biblicist on this question?
   *The reason he rejects this option is because when Scripture talks
   about it, it is consistently in terms of God doing it and not just
   permitting it.*

4. What are three examples given by Calvin?
   *He gives the example of Job's affliction, where the agent was Satan,
   but the ultimate decision was God's, as Job well knew. God willed
   that King Ahab be deceived, and a devil offers his services to this
   end. And the great example is that of Herod, Pilate, and all the Jews
   doing only what God determined they would do.*

[2]
Control of the Heart

1. Where does God's impulse to direct the wicked begin?
   Scripture describes Him working on their hearts.

2. Can God act on an agent in such a way that the agent acts himself?
   *Yes. This does not make God a puppet master. He is the ultimate
   reason these actions are performed, but those who do them remain
   responsible.*

3. Does Calvin give scriptural examples of God dealing directly with the
hearts of the wicked?
   *Yes, he gives multiple examples—Exodus 4:2; Psalm 105:25; 2 Thes-
   salonians 2:11; and Ezekiel 14:9.*

[3]
God's Manifold Will

1. What is the disposition behind a dismissal of God's complete sovereignty with a simple "to me it seems otherwise"?
   *A rebellious disposition which feels free to disregard the plain teach-
   ing of Scripture.*

2. Why do opponents of this doctrine claim that it makes have God possess two contrary wills?

If God decrees that something will happen, when His law prohibits that same thing, then this must mean God has two separate wills.

3. What is meant by God's "manifold" wisdom?

Calvin answers this by saying that God's will in itself is simple, but that because of our limitations it appears "manifold" to us.

[4]
God's Holy Disposition of All Things

1. What is the difference between God's decrees and God's commandments?

God can decree for something to happen when He has commanded us to not do it.

2. What is the difference between the Father's determination that Jesus die on the cross and the betrayal of Judas?

A good example of the decree/commandment distinction is the death of Jesus. Jesus was submitting to the will of the Father when He went to the cross (decree), but Judas was not therefore obeying God when he betrayed Jesus (commandment).

3. If this seems harsh to some readers, what does Calvin urge them to do?

Return to Scripture and consider how plainly this is taught there.

BOOK TWO

THE KNOWLEDGE OF GOD THE REDEEMER IN CHRIST

*First disclosed to the fathers under the law,
and then to us in the gospel*

—— CHAPTER ONE ——

· [1]

True Knowledge of Ourselves

1. What ancient proverb does Calvin commend?
   Know thyself.
2. What echo of an earlier point in Calvin does this make?
   Calvin begins the Institutes *by saying that man must know God and know himself.*
3. What are the two essential parts of self-knowledge?
   We must know the loftiness of our original estate, our "primal worthiness," and we must also know the magnitude of the Fall.

[2]

Deluded Self-Admiration

1. Instead of true self-knowledge, what do we tend to seek out instead?
   We seek out flattery.
2. What does this flattery appeal to?
   It appeals to the "pride that itches" in our "very marrow."

[3]

Gaining True Self-Knowledge

1. Does reflection on our original nobility create pride in us?
   No, just the opposite. It creates humility.

2. How are we then to divide our knowledge of ourselves?
We should meditate on the greatness of man's condition before the Fall, and we should weigh our own subsequent lack of ability to do anything right given the Fall.

3. What will this do?
It will cause us to cast ourselves upon God.

[4]

What Sin Is

1. Does Calvin believe that Adam was allowed to eat from the tree of life?
Yes.

2. Was Adam's sin simply gluttony?
No. What God so severely punished must have been "no light sin."

3. What was the root of Adam's sin?
Unfaithfulness.

4. What was the progress of Adam's rebellion?
Unfaithfulness led to pride and ambition, along with ingratitude, which resulted in disobedience.

[5]

Original Sin

1. How does Calvin define the "death of Adam's soul"?
He defines it as estrangement from God.

2. How does Calvin define "original sin"?
He defines it as "the depravation of a nature previously good and pure."

3. What was Pelagius' "profane fiction"?
It was that Adam sinned to his own hurt, and that his sin did not harm his descendants.

[6]

Is Original Sin Imitative?

1. When are children defiled by original sin?
At their begetting.

2. What is Adam's position with regard to the human race?
He is the "root of human nature."

3. What is, for Calvin, "beyond controversy"?
That if Christ's righteousness and life is ours by communication, then we receive sin and death from Adam the same way.

4. How does Calvin define that communication of righteousness from Christ?
As the power of righteousness being transfused into us.

[7]
Transmission of Sin

1. What should we be content to know with regard to all this?
That God gave to Adam what He intended the human race to have, and so when Adam lost those gifts, he lost them for us all.

2. Does the contagion spread through the substance of flesh or soul?
No. The contagion takes its origin because it has been so ordained by God.

[8]
Definition of Original Sin

1. How does Calvin define original sin?
As a hereditary depravity and corruption of our nature, diffused into all parts of the soul.

2. Do infants bear the curse of original sin?
Yes. Their "whole nature is a seed of sin."

3. Is this original sin nothing more than the absence of righteousness?
No, it includes the active presence of every evil.

[9]
The Whole Man in Sin

1. How far does original sin extend in a man?
To every part of his nature.

2. Is it true that the flesh is fallen, but the soul is not?
No. No part of a man remains "pure or untouched by that mortal disease."

[10]
Deranged Nature

1. What is Calvin's response to those who would write God's name upon their faults?
He calls them perverse and says, "Away with those persons."

2. What is wrong with asking the question "Why did God not prevent the Fall?"
It manifests inordinate curiosity.

[11]
Nature and Nature

1. In what way is sin unnatural?
It is contrary to the creational intent that God had in making man.
2. In what way is sin natural?
We call it natural because all men are in the grip of it by "hereditary right."

———— CHAPTER TWO ————

[1]
Miserable Servitude

1. What are the twin perils that threaten man, given his bondage to sin?
On the one hand, he becomes complacent because it is said that he cannot be righteous. On the other, if he resolves to attain to some moral stature himself, he robs God of His glory.
2. What does Augustine say that the defenders of free will do?
He says that they trample on free will more than they strengthen it.

[2]
The Philosophers' Optimism

1. What do the philosophers believe about reason?
That it is suffused with divine light, and that virtue depends upon following it.
2. Where do they believe our corruptions reside?
In our sense perceptions, in our physical nature.
3. Where do they locate the will?
Midway between reason and sense.

[3]
Freedom of Will

1. Do the philosophers believe that things can go wrong?
   Yes, certainly, as when a charioteer loses control of his chariot.

2. At the same time, do they believe that virtue is a real possibility?
   Yes, they do. Both virtue and vice are within our power.

3. According to Cicero, should we thank the gods for our own virtue?
   No, because virtue was our own contribution.

[4]
Church Fathers on Free Will

1. Does Calvin believe that the church fathers handled the idea of free will scripturally?
   No, he did not.

2. What was the reason for this?
   They tried to harmonize what they taught too closely with the teaching of the philosophers.

3. What two things were they concerned to avoid?
   They did not want to expose themselves to derision from the philosophers, and they did not want to seem to make room for moral slothfulness.

4. Which of the fathers was an exception to this?
   Augustine.

[5]
Different Kinds of Freedom

1. What were the three kinds of freedom that were distinguished in the schools?
   Freedom from necessity, freedom from sin, and freedom from misery.

2. Does Calvin accept this distinction?
   Yes, with the caveat that necessity not be muddled up with compulsion.

[6]
Cooperation with Grace

1. What is necessary before men can do good works truly?
   Only the elect receive this special grace through regeneration.

2. What ambiguity does Calvin object to in the teaching of Lombard?
   Calvin objected to the door that was opened to the idea that God offers grace, and we can either "render it ineffectual" by rejecting it or confirm it by "obediently following it."

[7]

Absence of Compulsion

1. What does Calvin think about "contentions about words"?
   He abhors them because their result is that the Church is harassed "to no purpose."
2. So why then does he reject the words "free will" so strongly?
   Because it is virtually impossible to use the phrase without encouraging a "ruinous self-assurance."

[8]

Augustine on Free Will

1. What does Augustine teach about the will?
   He teaches that "man's will is not free" unless the Spirit has brought that freedom.
2. Does Augustine use the phrase "free will"?
   Yes, but in a way that mocks "its empty name."
3. What is Calvin's approach to the phrase?
   He prefers not to use it and advises others not to use it either.

[9]

Conflicted Voices among the Fathers

1. What is the problem with the other fathers?
   Sometimes they exalt free will. Other times they give all the glory to Christ. Calvin objects to their inconsistency.
2. What does Calvin say in their favor?
   That however excessive they are in "extolling free will," their intent was to "teach man utterly to forsake confidence in his own virtue."

[10]

Refusing to Rob God

1. When a man is utterly cast down in himself, what has he gained?
   True knowledge of himself.

2. What is the problem with a man retaining to himself some of the honor found in "free will"?
It usurps God of His honor and is monstrous sacrilege.

3. Who may receive God's blessings?
One who is consumed with an awareness of his own poverty.

[11]

True Humility

1. What did Augustine say were the three chief rules for eloquence?
Delivery, delivery, delivery.

2. In a similar vein, what does Calvin say are the three chief precepts of the Christian religion?
Humility, humility, humility.

3. Instead of relying on human nature, which is "wounded, battered, troubled" and "lost," what do we need?
We need true confession, not false defense.

4. In order for our war with God to be over, what must happen?
We must be unarmed. Our weapons of impiety must be "shattered, broken, and burned."

[12]

The Fall Described

1. In the Fall, what happened to our supernatural gifts like faith and righteousness?
We lost them completely.

2. What happened to our natural gifts, like soundness of mind and uprightness of heart?
They were corrupted.

3. Have we fallen to the level of the brute beasts?
No. The "misshapen ruins" of our natural gifts still appear.

[13]

Two Kinds of Understanding

1. What are the two kinds of understanding according to Calvin?
Understanding of earthly things and understanding of heavenly things.

2. What is included in the former?
Matters involved with the present life, like government, household management, mechanical skill, and the liberal arts.

3. The latter?
Pure knowledge of God, the nature of true righteousness, and the mysteries of the heavenly kingdom.

[14]

Understanding Arts and Science

1. What does virtually every human being possess?
Talent in some art.

2. What do we learn from imbeciles?
Gratitude, because we see how much God has left to us.

3. What is a natural gift?
One bestowed on the pious and the impious alike.

[15]

Knowledge as God's Gift

1. If we regard the Spirit of God as the sole fountain of truth, what follows?
We will not reject truth, no matter where it first appears.

2. What should our response be to the great accomplishments of un-believers?
Great admiration.

[16]

The Spirit's Work

1. What do we learn from Bezalel and Oholiab?
That the Spirit works to bestow understanding and knowledge in the arts and sciences.

2. Is the Spirit's work limited to believers?
No. Apart from His work in sanctifying believers, He also fills, moves, and quickens all things, and He does so in accordance with the law of creation.

[17]

A Summary

1. What is proper to our nature?
Reason.

2. What must we avoid claiming as our own?
That which flows from the sheer bounty of God.

[18]

Limits of Understanding

1. What are the three characteristics of spiritual insight?
   Knowing God, knowing His fatherly favor toward us, and knowing how to frame our lives according to His law.

2. What illustration does Calvin use to describe unbelievers when they have a true insight concerning God?
   They are like a traveler in the field at night who sees everything lit up by a flash of lightning, but who is then immediately in the dark again.

[19]

Spiritual Blindness

1. Do unbelievers have some illumination concerning God?
   Yes, but not enough to comprehend Him.

2. How do we know men do not have spiritual understanding?
   Because John 1 describes men as "darkness."

[20]

God's Work in Man

1. How do men regain what nature lacks?
   We regain what we have lost through the Spirit of regeneration.

2. How far may a man become spiritually wise?
   Only as far as God illumines a man's mind.

[21]

The Light of the Spirit

1. Where the Spirit of God does not shine, what do we have?
   Only darkness.

2. What is the worst form of blindness?
   Not knowing yourself to be blind.

[22]

What Natural Law Is For

1. Does Calvin take the Gentiles in Romans 2:14–15 to be Christians or not?
   He takes them as unbelieving Gentiles.

2. Does Calvin believe in natural law?
   Yes, he does.

3. How does he define it?
   As the apprehension of the conscience which distinguishes just from unjust.

4. What is natural law for?
   It removes the excuse of ignorance.

[23]
General and Particular

1. Can unregenerate men affirm the right ethical choice generally?
   Yes, they can.

2. Where then do they fail, according to Calvin?
   They fail in the particulars concerning their own life. They know adultery is wrong, but have rationalizations for their own adultery.

[24]
First and Second Table

1. Where does human ethical knowledge fail utterly?
   With regard to the duties found in the First Table of the Law.

2. Where does it fail in a critical sense?
   In attempts to obey the Second Table of the Law, human efforts are plagued by lack of endurance, by inconsistency of application, and by failure to take our concupiscence into account.

3. What do the philosophers recognize and what do they ignore?
   They recognize gross sins, but they ignore "the evil desires that gently tickle the mind."

[25]
Absolute Depravity?

1. Does Calvin hold that men are evil in every respect?
   No. Otherwise how could that which is pleasing to God even enter our minds?

2. But what is absolutely necessary in order for us to understand spiritual things?
   The grace of illumination, and to be reborn as David was.

[26]
More on Free Will

1. Choice belongs to what sphere in our makeup?
   It belongs to the sphere of the will, not the understanding.

2. What is necessary before we can say that a true moral choice has been made?
   That a man discern the good by right reason, that he choose it while knowing what it is, and that, having chosen it, he follows it.

[27]
The Need for the Holy Spirit

1. Does Calvin believe that the description in Romans 7 is of a Christian or not?
   He holds that it is the self-description of a Christian.

2. What does he make of the excuse "I myself do not do evil, but sin that dwells in me"?
   He holds that only a regenerate man could say that.

--------- CHAPTER THREE ---------

[1]
All Is Flesh

1. Is all of man's nature fleshly?
   Yes, and this is why no good can be extracted from it.

2. What is the only way to obtain anything of spiritual value from the Spirit?
   By regeneration.

3. Whatever we have from nature is what?
   Flesh.

[2]
A Witness to Corruption

1. What passage does Paul turn to in order to throw down the arrogance of mankind?
   Romans 3:10–16.

2. Is this passage limited to some men?
   No, it applies to the whole race of Adam's children.

3. What are the two reasons men are this way?
   They are this way not only because of depraved custom, but also by depravity of nature.

[3]
Limited Grace

1. Does Calvin agree that some unbelievers have some nobility in their nature?
   Yes. Depravity is total, but not absolute.

2. How does Calvin account for this?
   By saying that God gives enough grace to restrain sin inwardly, but not so much as to cleanse it.

[4]
God's Gift of Virtue

1. Does Calvin agree that we must make "Camillus equal to Cataline"?
   Yes, but only if we refuse to acknowledge that carefully cultivated nature can be capable of goodness.

2. Which way does Calvin take it?
   He says that cultivated nature is capable of some good.

3. How?
   By means of "special graces" that God gives.

4. Do these virtues put these men in a right standing with God?
   No, because the chief part of uprightness is still absent.

[5]
Necessity, Not Compulsion

1. We must attribute conversion entirely to what?
   Entirely to God's grace.

2. What drives evil will, and what drives good will?
   A corrupt nature drives evil will, and grace drives a good will.

3. Those who are offended by this do not know how to do what?
   They do not know how to distinguish necessity from compulsion.

4. If necessity is the same as compulsion, what must be said about God?
   That He is good under compulsion.

5. Calvin agrees with whom in these matters?
With Augustine, and the agreement of all the godly.

[6]

Effectual Grace

1. What must we not divide?
We must not divide between God and ourselves what He claims for Himself alone.

[7]

Imagined Cooperation

1. What does Calvin think of Lombard's idea of "prevenient grace"?
Not much. He says that Lombard "preposterously twisted" a saying of Augustine to get there.

2. What is prior to all merit?
Grace.

[8]

Scriptural Foundations

1. Why does Calvin cite Augustine?
To answer those who claim that Calvin is twisting Scripture.

2. What is the basis for Calvin's assertions on this topic?
Calvin says that this teaching has been drawn from Scripture.

3. How do we know that faith is a free gift of God?
The whole of Scripture proclaims it.

[9]

Our Blessedness from God Alone

1. What antithesis must we always remember?
The antithesis between the perverse motions of disobedience and the correction of God.

2. How does Calvin describe the license of our pride?
As strange and monstrous.

[10]
Not Just Possibilities

1. Does God's grace give us a chance to be good or not?
   No. Grace disposes efficaciously.

2. What must we not claim?
   The slightest part of God's praise.

[11]
Perseverance All of God

1. What is perseverance *not?*
   It is not distributed as a reward for good use of earlier grace.

2. Is grace a co-worker with us?
   No. Those who think of grace as a "partner" are wretchedly deluding themselves.

[12–13]
Not One Good Work

1. Can man take credit for even one good work apart from grace?
   No, not at all.

2. What, according to Augustine, brings about every good work in us?
   Grace alone.

[14]
Is the Will Eradicated?

1. Does grace eliminate the will?
   No. The will is changed from evil to good and helped when it is good.

2. What is the right relationship of grace and freedom?
   The human will does not obtain grace by freedom, but rather freedom by grace.

CHAPTER FOUR

[1]

Willingly under the Devil's Power

1. Does man sin willingly, even though of necessity?
   Yes. He sins under necessity, not under compulsion.

2. What comparison of Augustine's does Calvin approve?
   That of a horse and rider. Man is the horse, and the rider is God or Satan respectively.

[2]

In the Same Event

1. Who was involved in Job's loss?
   God, Satan, and the Chaldeans.

2. What distinguishes these various agents?
   First the end and then the manner of acting.

3. What aspect of God's sovereignty is Calvin not addressing here?
   His universal activity whereby creatures are enabled to do anything at all.

[3]

Hardness

1. Why do the early fathers not want to attribute "hardening" to God?
   They are concerned the impious will speak of it blasphemously.

2. What does Calvin think of this?
   He sympathizes but says that Scripture does not speak this way.

3. What does Calvin call the idea that hardening is nothing but permission or a matter of foreknowledge?
   He calls it a subtlety that Scripture does not admit.

4. Considering the editor's footnote, how does Calvin chide Augustine unnecessarily?
   He accepted as genuine a work attributed to Augustine that was not his.

[4]

God's Treatment of the Godless

1. Are there passages that describe God as acting on the godless by simply "deserting" them?

Yes, there are.

2. Does this explanation cover all the scriptural data?

No, there are "other testimonies that go beyond these," describing God as actively hardening.

[5]

Satan Controlled

1. What error must be avoided when discussing the "evil spirit from the Lord"?

This spirit must not be confounded with the Holy Spirit.

2. Can God and Satan work in the same man at the same time?

Yes, but to different ends.

[6]

Sovereignty over "Neutral" Actions

1. When actions are neither good nor evil, is God still involved?

Yes. God is sovereign in all things.

[7]

Control of Kings

1. How is God's control of kingly actions (Prov. 21:1) a "how much more" argument?

If any man might be expected to be free to do as he wishes, a king would be. And if God controls him, how much more everyone else?

[8]

Controlling What We Want

1. For Calvin, is free will to be determined by whether or not a man chooses what he wants?

No. The question is internal to the man and is not a matter of outcomes.

—————— CHAPTER FIVE ——————

[1]

First Objection

1. What is the first objection to Calvin's teaching on free will?
   That in order to be sin at all, an action must be voluntary. Necessary sin is not sin.

2. How do his opponents support this objection?
   By means of "common sense" and certain scriptural arguments.

3. How does Calvin answer?
   By distinguishing (again) necessity and compulsion. The fact that it occurs necessarily does not mean it occurs involuntarily.

[2]

Second Objection

1. What is the second objection to Calvin's teaching on free will?
   That the loss of free will means that reward and punishment lose their meaning.

2. How does Calvin answer?
   He answers with a solid dose from Augustine. Scripture teaches that God rewards the grace He gives, so that sins are our own, while our virtues are gifts from God.

[3]

Third Objection

1. What is the third objection to Calvin's teaching on free will?
   That this obliterates all distinction between good and evil.

2. How does Calvin answer?
   He answers what he considers to be a closely related point, one concerning perseverance. He says that some persevere and some do not because God upholds those who do and does not uphold those who do not.

[4]

Fourth Objection

1. What is the fourth objection to Calvin's teaching on free will?
   That all exhortation becomes meaningless.

2. How does Calvin answer?
Again with an appeal to Augustine, followed by citations from the Bible. The basic answer is that this is a scriptural doctrine, and yet Scripture is full of exhortation. Therefore there is no inconsistency.

[5]

Why Exhortation?

1. If an impious man scoffs at exhortations from God, what can he not do?
He cannot condemn those exhortations.

2. What rests entirely upon God's grace?
All the righteousness of the pious.

3. In what two ways docs God work upon His elect?
He works within by His Spirit, and He works from without by His word.

[6]

The Central Objection

1. What is the central objection to Calvin's views of free will?
That God's precepts must indicate the measure of our strength.

2. Do his opponents have no Scripture at all?
They have a host of passages, all of them misunderstood.

3. How does Calvin state this objection?
By saying that God is either mocking us when He enjoins personal holiness, or He is requiring only what is within our power to do.

[7]

The Answer

1. If the law does not show what we ought to do and are able to do, what does it show?
It reveals our condition of sinfulness. It reveals that we are unable to do what is right.

[8]

The Answer from Scripture

1. How has Calvin broken up this particular objection?
Into three categories—the commands to be converted, the commands to honor God, and the commands to remain in God's grace.

2. What does he then do with these categories?
He shows various scriptural passages in each category that show God giving to His people what He has commanded them to do.

[9]
Not a Shared Work

1. How is the work of conversion divided between God and man?
It is not divided.

2. When God gives His law, what can we say about the grace of the Lawgiver?
That it is both necessary and promised to us.

[10]
Empty Promises?

1. To whom are the promises offered?
To the impious and believers alike.

2. What effect do the promises have on the impious?
They prick the conscience, showing them how unworthy they are of His continued kindnesses.

3. What effect do the promises have on the believers?
Since our sluggishness is not sufficiently aroused by His precepts, He gives us promises to sweetly entice us to love the precepts.

[11]
The Meaning of Reproof

1. Why can unbelievers not find fault with God for His reproof of them?
Because they must find the source of the evil within themselves, and not from external causes.

[12]
The Word Is Near You

1. How does Calvin interpret Deuteronomy 30:11–12, 14?
With reference to the interpretation Paul gives it in Romans 10.

2. And what interpretation is that?
The words in Deuteronomy, according to Paul, apply to the gospel and not to the law.

[13]

When God Waits

1. What is the next objection that Calvin deals with?
   The objection is that if God waits for men to respond, this must mean that they can respond, one way or the other.

2. How does Calvin answer this?
   By saying that Scripture elsewhere teaches that men who are forsaken by God cannot do right. And if his opponents say that grace is necessary, then what is the problem?

[14]

Our Works

1. What objection is addressed in this section?
   The objection is that the Bible calls righteous works of men "our works."

2. How does Calvin answer?
   By pointing out that the bread God gives us in response to the Lord's Prayer is called "our daily bread." It is ours because God gave it to us.

[15]

Shared Possession

1. In what sense are our good works ours, and in what sense God's?
   They are ours because they were a gift to us, and God's because He gave them.

[16]

Cain and Abel

1. What is the next objection?
   That God tells Cain that he must master sin. This must mean that he could.

2. What is Calvin's view of this passage?
   He says the verse applies to Abel. But for the sake of argument he supposes that it speaks of sin and says it is either command or promise. If command, he has dealt with this earlier. If promise, why was the promise not fulfilled?

[17]
Straining for Something

1. What argument for free will is drawn from Romans 9:16?
   That if it is not of him who wills and of him who runs, willing and running must have some kind of place.

2. What word does Calvin use in dismissing this argument?
   "Away then with these subtleties."

[18]
Ecclesiasticus

1. Does Calvin reject the author of Ecclesiasticus?
   Surprisingly, no. Although he says that he has the right to.

2. How does he handle this appeal?
   By interpreting Ecclesiasticus in an orthodox way—although he doesn't have to. The book is not in the canon of Scripture, so it could be just wrong.

3. What does man need instead of an advocate?
   A physician.

[19]
Half Alive

1. How does Calvin handle the allegorical argument from the fact that the man beat up on the Jericho road was "half alive"?
   He rejects the allegory.

2. What ought allegories not be allowed to do, according to Calvin?
   They ought not go beyond the limits set by the rule of Scripture, and they should not be used as the foundation of any doctrine.

3. And how does Calvin handle the assertion that mankind is "half alive"?
   By pointing to the Scriptures which describe sinners as dead.

CHAPTER SIX

[1]

The Need for a Mediator

1. What illustration does Calvin use to describe heaven and earth?
    He calls it "this magnificent theater" and says that it is crammed with innumerable miracles.

2. What is our problem then?
    Looking at these wonders, we ought to have known God. But because of sin, we do not.

3. What does God do for us in this situation?
    He calls us to the faith of Christ—we need a Mediator, a Redeemer.

4. Has any worship apart from Christ ever pleased God?
    No, not at all.

[2]

Even in the Old Covenant

1. Is the need for a Mediator revealed to us for the first time in the New Testament?
    No. The doctrine is found throughout the Old Testament as well.

2. In order to be propitious toward the human race, what does God need?
    God needs a Mediator in order to save us.

[3]

Always Christ

1. When is Christ prefigured in the Old Testament?
    Whenever solace is promised in affliction, especially when the deliverance of the Church is in view.

2. In the Old Testament, on what did our redemption and eternal salvation depend?
    On the coming kingdom of David.

3. The hope of all the godly has always reposed where?
    In Christ alone.

[4]

Faith in God Alone Is Insufficient

1. What will happen to someone's faith in God without a Mediator?
It will gradually disappear.

2. Why can we not attain to God's majesty?
It is too lofty, and we are like grubs crawling on the earth.

3. What teaching of Paul's should have been more commonly known among the Jews?
That Christ was the end of the law.

4. Are Muslims true theists because they worship one God?
No, because without a Mediator they are idolaters.

———— CHAPTER SEVEN ————

[1]

The Meaning of Law

1. What does Calvin mean when he uses the word "law"?
The form of religion delivered to Moses.

2. What was the basic reason for giving the law?
To set the people's mind on Christ, to kindle a desire for Him.

[2]

The End of the Law

1. What should we remember with regard to the Ten Commandments?
That Christ is the end of the law for the one who believes.

2. The righteousness taught by the commandments is all in vain until what happens?
Until Christ confers that righteousness by free imputation and by the Spirit of regeneration.

[3]

More on the Law

1. What else does the law do?
It renders us inexcusable and drives us into despair.

2. How many men are affected by the law in this way?
All of us, to a man.

[4]
Promises

1. Are the promises attached to the law all in vain because of our disobedience?
   Not at all. The promises make us realize they will not be fulfilled unless God does the fulfilling.

[5]
The Meaning of Impossible

1. What does Calvin mean by the impossibility of obedience?
   He means something is impossible when it has never been, and what God's ordination and decree prevent from ever being.

2. What has plagued every human being?
   Concupiscence.

3. What ought we not pit against one another?
   God's power and God's truth.

[6]
Removing Self-Deception

1. Without seeing ourselves in the mirror of God's law, what happens to us?
   Drunk with self-love, we deceive ourselves.

2. When we stand on our own judgment, what do we tend to do?
   Pass off hypocrisy as righteousness.

[7]
Reflective Law

1. The law is compared to what?
   The law is like a mirror, showing us our sins the way a mirror shows us the spots on our face.

2. As we grow tired under the burden of sin, what does God never tire of?
   He never tires of benefitting us and heaping new gifts upon us.

[8]
First Use of the Law Universal

1. Does the first use of the law apply to unbelievers only?
   No, it works upon believers and unbelievers both.

[9]

Motivation

1. When we are condemned by the law, what does this make us want to do?
   It makes us desire to call upon the grace of God's help.

[10]

The Second Use

1. What is the second use of the law?
   To restrain the public ungodliness of the wicked.

2. Is their conformity to this law true righteousness?
   No, but this constrained and forced righteousness is necessary for any public community of men.

[11]

Restraint for a Time

1. The law of God restrains us externally until what time?
   Until we are regenerated by the Spirit and begin wholeheartedly to love Him.

[12]

The Third Use

1. What is the third use of the law, according to Calvin?
   It provides admonition to believers and exhorts them in living a life of love.

2. Is this a minor use of the law?
   No, it is the principal use.

3. How does the law help the believer?
   It is a spur to doing right.

4. Is this use dependent upon precept alone?
   No. Grace sweetens what is bitter.

[13]

Antinomianism

1. What do certain ignorant persons do?
   They cast out the whole law of Moses.

[14]

Abrogation

1. In what two ways has the law been abrogated?
   With regard to the sting of conscience and through the discontinuance of the ceremonies.

[15]

Conscience

1. What part of the law is abrogated to liberate the conscience?
   The part of the law that enforces its precepts—the thunderbolt of the curse.

2. How would that curse work on the conscience?
   Through fear of death.

[16]

The Ceremonies

1. Have the ceremonies been abrogated the same way?
   No, not at all.

2. In what way have the ceremonies been abrogated?
   They have been abrogated, not in effect, but only in their use.

[17]

The Written Bond

1. What does Calvin do with the "written bond" of Colossians 2:13–14?
   He applies it to the ceremonies, provided those ceremonies are understood as a confession of sin.

—————— CHAPTER EIGHT ——————

[1]

Natural Law Written

1. What is the written moral law?
   It is a written statement of the natural law.

2. What does God reprove us for through the law?
   For our impotence and for our unrighteousness.

3. Why is the written law necessary?
To make the force of natural law in our conscience more plain and to provide a clearer witness.

[2]
Inexorable Law

1. When do we render God the reverence due to Him?
When we prefer His will to our own.

2. In what way is God always like Himself?
As the friend of righteousness, as the foe of iniquity.

[3]
Learning about Ourselves

1. What does the law teach us about ourselves?
Two things: first, our comparative unrighteousness, and secondly, our impotence to fulfill the law.

[4]
Promises and Threats

1. Why has God added promises and threats to the law?
In order to stir up in us a love of righteousness and a hatred of wickedness.

2. What deserves no reward?
The payment of a debt.

[5]
The Law's Sufficiency

1. Nothing is more acceptable to God than what?
Obedience.

2. What religious affectation is rooted in man's nature?
To dream up religious rites in order to deserve well of God.

3. What is an intolerable profanation of divine righteousness?
Any zeal for good works that wanders outside God's law.

[6]
Total Law

1. If an earthly king forbids a particular action, what is not included?
   The heart attitudes involved.

2. How is this different from what God forbids?
   God searches out the heart, and so He evaluates that as well.

[7]
Christ and the Law

1. Who is the best interpreter of the law?
   Christ Himself.

2. Did Christ add to the law?
   No, He restored it to its original integrity.

[8]
Right Meaning

1. Does a refusal to go beyond the law require that we interpret the law woodenly?
   No, the law must not be interpreted according to "narrowness of words" but must allow for figures of speech.

2. What is our central duty with regard to each law?
   We must investigate what it is concerned with in the first place.

[9]
The Flip Side of the Law

1. What is conceded by all?
   That if a virtue is commanded, then the corresponding vice is prohibited, and vice versa.

2. What mistake is commonly made in this?
   That if, for example, murder is prohibited, I have fulfilled the law if I simply refrain from murder. But Calvin says this entails that we give our neighbor's life all the help we can.

[10]

Strong Language

1. Why does God rebuke sin so strongly in the law and put the worst possible light on our behavior? For example, why call hatred "murder"?
   Because we tend to gloss all of our sins. God intends to teach us to detest sin rightly.

[11]

Two Tables

1. How does Calvin divide the law given in the Ten Commandments?
   Into two sections—the first having to do with our duties to God, the second having to do with our duties to man.

2. What is vanity to attempt?
   To cry up righteousness without religion—to praise righteousness toward men without a right relation to God.

[12]

Right Division

1. Why do some number the commandments differently?
   In order to get the prohibition of image worship into the background somehow.

[13]

The Preface

1. How does Calvin take the preface to the Ten Commandments?
   As the preface to the entire law.

2. Why is the preface important?
   Because it highlights and underscores the nature of the God who gives the commandments.

[14]

The Meaning of the Name

1. What is meant by "I am Jehovah your God"?
   By this phrase God declares Himself to be God of the Church. He is emphasizing that He is our God, and we are His people.

[15]

Out of Bondage

1. What does Calvin identify as one of the greatest crimes?
   The crime of ingratitude.

2. Why does God reveal Himself through certain particular titles?
   To restrain us from inventing absurdities about Him.

3. What did Israel's enslavement in Israel represent typologically?
   Our slavery to sin, and so the motivation to godliness in the preface applies to us as well.

[16]

Authority

1. What does the first commandment reveal about God's authority?
   That His authority is complete and total.

2. What four things may we not transfer away from God to another?
   Adoration, trust, invocation, and thanksgiving.

[17]

The Grossest Fault

1. What is the grossest fault of a superstitious style of worship?
   Outward idolatry.

2. What happens whenever idols appear?
   True religion is corrupted and adulterated.

[18]

Warnings about Idolatry

1. Penalties for idolatry extend how far?
   To children, grandchildren, and great-grandchildren.

2. How far does His kindness extend to those who love Him and keep His word?
   To thousands of generations or, as Calvin phrases it, to remote posterity.

3. What is the act of bowing down to an image compared to?
   To the act of adultery.

[19]
Visiting Iniquity

1. Does Calvin interpret the threat to "visit iniquity" to subsequent generations as a reference to temporal difficulties only?
   No. He grants that it does happen, but he insists that it encompasses spiritual judgments as well.

[20]
Justice and Generational Judgment

1. Why did Ezekiel tell the people to stop using the proverb about the father eating grapes and the children's teeth being set on edge?
   Because Israelites were using it to describe a wicked father and a son experiencing consequences, a son who was "otherwise righteous."
2. What therefore descends to subsequent generations?
   Not only the judgment, but also the sin. It does not accord with God's justice for "a righteous son to pay the penalty of a wicked father."

[21]
Mercy to Thousands

1. How is this promise to be interpreted? As an absolute, or as a general rule?
   As a general rule. The offspring of the wicked sometimes repent, and the children of the righteous sometimes fall away.

[22]
The Third Commandment

1. What does the third commandment require?
   That we hallow the majesty of God's name.
2. What three things constitute adherence to this command?
   First, everything we think, say, or do should "savor of His excellence"; second, we must not rashly abuse His word or His mysteries; and third, we must not defame or detract from His works.

[23]
The Meaning of an Oath

1. What is an oath?
   It is calling God to witness the truth of our word.

2. What is one way of identifying a man's religion?
By the name he uses in taking an oath.

[24]

True Name and False Word

1. What is it when a man swears falsely in the true name?
It is no small affront; it is what Scripture calls a "profanation."

[25]

Idle Oaths

1. What renders God's name cheap and common?
When it is invoked for true but needless oaths.

2. When men swear unnecessarily, what are they doing?
They are departing from its lawful use.

[26]

Sermon on the Mount

1. Who condemns all oaths whatever, and why?
The Anabaptists, on the basis of a mistake concerning Christ's words in the Sermon on the Mount.

2. Interpreting Christ's words as forbidding all oaths whatever does what to the relationship between Jesus and His Father?
It makes Christ His Father's enemy, because God permitted and sometimes required oaths.

3. What was Christ forbidding then?
He is forbidding the form of oaths that He uses as illustrations. He is "refuting the wily sophistry of those who see nothing wrong in idly tossing about indirect oaths."

4. What is the relationship of God's name to all His benefits?
His name is actually engraven on all His benefits.

[27]

More on Oaths

1. Did Paul interpret Jesus as forbidding all oaths?
No, he swears without hesitation, sometimes even adding a curse.

[28]

The Sabbath

1. What did Calvin think about the early fathers who interpreted the Sabbath as a type of Christ?
He says that they spoke truly, but that they did not go far enough.

2. What are the three elements of obedience to this command?
First, it represents spiritual rest. Second, there is a need for a particular day to hear the law and perform the appointed rites. And third, a day is necessary to give rest to those under authority.

[29]

The Chief Place

1. What lesson occupied the chief place in the Sabbath?
The foreshadowing of spiritual rest.

2. When should we be at this place of spiritual rest?
All the time.

[30]

The Seventh Day

1. What does the number seven represent in Scripture?
It is the number of perfection and denotes perpetuity.

[31]

Sabbath Fulfillment

1. Can the Sabbath be kept merely by abstaining from physical labor?
No. The prophets repeatedly refer to this.

2. What must Christians shun completely?
Because the substance of the shadow belongs to Christ, Christians ought to completely shun superstitious observance of days.

[32]

What Remains

1. For Calvin, the Sabbath has been abrogated in Christ. But what two things do we still need to do?
We still need to gather on stated days to hear the word, break the mystical bread, and conduct public prayers. We also need to give relief to servants and workmen.

[33]

Superstition

1. Is there danger in Christian superstitious observance of the Lord's day?
   Yes, but less than there is for the observance of Jewish holy days.

[34]

Why Sunday?

1. For Calvin, is the Lord's day a continuation of the Sabbath or a replacement of it?
   It is a replacement. Calvin is not a sabbatarian.
2. Why was the first day chosen as that replacement?
   Because Jesus rose from the dead on that day.
3. Does Calvin condemn churches that have other solemn days?
   No, he does not—provided there is no superstition.

[35]

The Wide Meaning of Honor

1. Who is encompassed under the fifth commandment?
   Anyone that God has placed over us.
2. Is honor a word with a narrow definition?
   No, in Scripture it has a very broad meaning.
3. What do fathers, princes, and lords all have?
   A share in God's honor.

[36]

Worthy of Honor

1. Are we allowed to withhold honor based on the recipient's lack of merit?
   No, it makes no difference whether they are worthy of it or not.
2. What are the three components of honor?
   Reverence, obedience, and gratitude.

[37]

Commandment with a Promise

1. Does the promise attached to this commandment apply to us today?
   Yes, this "promise similarly has reference to us."

2. With the "exceptions," is God breaking His word?
*No, no more than if He gave a man a hundred acres when He had
promised him one.*

[38]

The Threat

1. Are there sanctions connected to this commandment?
Yes, an inevitable curse awaits all stubborn or disobedient children.

[39]

The Sixth Commandment

1. What is the purpose of this commandment?
*Because God has bound all humanity together in a certain unity,
each man must concern himself with the safety of all.*
2. What is hatred?
Nothing but sustained anger.
3. Does this command address heart attitudes?
*Yes, because the God who sees the heart does not issue commands
solely to the body.*

[40]

Twin Reasons

1. What are the two reasons we are to refrain from murder?
*Because all men bear the image of God, and because we share a
common flesh with all men.*

[41]

Calvin on Adultery

1. Why should all uncleanness be far from us?
Because God loves modesty and purity.
2. What effect does fornication have?
It brands our bodies with its mark.

[42]

Celibate Follies

1. What makes men doubly subject to women's society?
Our created nature and the effects of the Fall.

2. What two ways is the gift of celibacy given?
It is granted entirely to a few and to others just for a time.

3. Why can men not count on God's help for any attempt at celibacy?
Because God helps only those who walk in His ways.

[43]

Marriage

1. Can celibacy be achieved by great zeal and effort?
No, it has to be a special grace from God.

2. If a man is not able to be celibate, what does God require of him?
That he marry.

3. Is it adequate for a man to control external sexual behavior?
No, a true celibate knows how to be pure in body and spirit both.

[44]

Chastity within Marriage

1. What can we say about sexual association within marriage?
That it is blessed by the Lord.

2. What follows from this?
That married couples ought not to give way to uncontrolled lust.

3. Is anything permitted, just so long as the couple is married?
No, there are a number of practices unworthy of the marriage bed that would exhibit extreme lewdness.

[45]

Prohibition of Theft

1. What is the eighth commandment?
That we honor the possessions of others.

2. What is prohibited in this commandment?
The evil deprivation of another's possessions.

3. Does it matter if we figure out a way to do it legally?
No, a court action cannot cleanse the guilt of a theft.

[46]

Love and Property

1. What sort of gain should we pursue?
Only that which is lawful and honest.

2. What do greedy men look like?
They madly scrape together from everywhere, by fair means or foul.

3. What should we do if we have to contend with faithless and deceitful men?
Give up something rather than contend with them.

[47]

Ninth Commandment

1. What is the ninth commandment?
That we refrain from false witness against our neighbor.

2. What is the first form of this that Calvin mentions?
Maligning him with false or slanderous charges.

3. For Calvin, what are the two parts of this commandment?
That we refrain from injuring a man's reputation, and that we refrain from depriving him of his goods by lying.

[48]

Good Reputation

1. What peculiar temptation does everyone experience in this regard?
We all tend to delight in a certain poisoned sweetness in ferreting out and disclosing the evils of others.

2. What is not included under this prohibition?
Private or public correction meant to remedy the evil.

3. What else is excluded?
Bitter taunts under the guise of joking.

[49]

Ten Commandment

1. What is the tenth commandment?
That we not covet anything whatever that belongs to our neighbor.

2. If the prohibitions of adultery and murder forbade heart intent, then how is this commandment not superfluous?
Calvin distinguishes an intent to do something from a prickling or tickling with that desire. This commandment is therefore functioning at a much higher internal plane.

[50]
Inmost Righteousness

1. What happens if we entertain any desirable object in our minds?
   Our hearts leap with excitement.
2. What does God require of our heart?
   He requires a marvelously tempered heart, not allowing the tiniest pinprick of anything that is not love.

[51]
The Sum of the Law

1. What is the purpose of the whole law?
   To form human life to the archetype of divine purity.
2. What is a mistake to believe concerning the law?
   That it is simply the rudiments or preliminaries of righteousness.

[52]
The Second Table

1. Why is the keeping of the law sometimes summarized in the second table only?
   Because it is speaking of that by which a man proves himself righteous.
2. What are the two indicators of keeping the first table?
   Heart condition and keeping the ceremonies.
3. Why is this inadequate for identifying true godliness?
   Because only God sees the heart, and hypocrites busy themselves with ceremonies. And so we tell who loves God by who loves his neighbor.

[53]
Fulfillment

1. What is the fulfillment of the law?
   He who loves his neighbor fulfills the law.

[54]
Love of Neighbor

1. What life best conforms to God's will?
   A life that is most fruitful for its brethren.
2. What stupid imagination did the Sophists advance?
   That self-love was of first importance.

3. How does Calvin refute this?
By pointing out that God was simply using a given from the midst of our depravity and by citing 1 Corinthians 13:5. Love does not seek its own.

[55]

Who Is Our Neighbor?

1. Does Calvin resist the priorities we have for those closest to us?
No, this does not offend God. His own providence leads us to it.

2. Does love for a man depend on his character?
No, it depends on our love for God.

[56]

The Schoolmen's Distortions

1. What did the Schoolmen do with all these divine requirements?
They turned them into mere "counsels," obligatory for monks only.

2. How did Calvin respond?
With scorn and multiple citations of Scripture.

[57]

Real Commandments

1. How was the command to love our enemies diluted by some?
By making the instructions in how to love exhortations, not imperatives.

2. What early church fathers did Calvin appeal to in rejecting this?
Chrysostom and Augustine.

[58]

Mortal and Venial Sins

1. What is the definition of venial sin that Calvin works with?
The definition from Aquinas—"Desire without deliberate assent, which does not long remain in the heart."

2. But how do these sins even get an opportunity within us?
Because of some empty place in the soul—we were already not loving God with all our heart, soul, mind, and strength.

3. So what does all sin deserve?
All sin deserves death.

[59]

Every Sin Deadly

1. Why is every sin deadly?
   Because every sin sets God's authority aside.

2. If those who distinguish mortal from venial sin "persist in their ravings," what should we do?
   Bid them farewell.

3. What should the children of God hold?
   That all sin is mortal.

—————— CHAPTER NINE ——————

[1]

A Foretaste

1. What did God attest through the Old Testament promises?
   That He was Father.

2. What did the teaching and ceremonies of the Old Testament point to?
   They all pointed to Christ.

3. Did this make this teaching valueless to the prophets themselves?
   Not at all—they enjoyed a slight taste of what we possess.

[2]

Two Senses of Gospel

1. Taken in a broad sense, what does the word "gospel" include?
   It includes the testimonies God gave to the patriarchs of old.

2. Taken in the higher sense, what does it mean?
   It refers to the proclamation of grace manifested in Christ.

[3]

Promises for Us

1. Are the promises of the Old Testament abrogated with the law?
   No, contrary to the teaching of Servetus.

[4]
Law and Gospel

1. For Calvin, is there a legitimate contrast between law and gospel?
   Yes, provided the contrast is not made too sharply.

2. Did the gospel bring a different way of salvation than the law, rightly understood?
   No. The gospel confirmed and satisfied what the law had promised.

[5]
John the Baptist

1. What kind of office did John the Baptist hold with regard to law and gospel?
   An intermediate office.

2. What was his role with regard to the disciples?
   To prepare the disciples for Christ.

———— CHAPTER TEN ————

[1]
A Unified Covenant

1. What point does Calvin believe is very important to make?
   That all men adopted into the company of God's people throughout the history of the world have had the same law and the same doctrine.

2. What was said concerning the Jews by Calvin's opponents?
   In effect that they were nothing but a herd of swine, being fattened on this earth with worldly pleasures only.

[2]
Points of Unity

1. How much alike are the various covenants that God has made with men?
   So much alike in substance and reality that they are actually one and the same.

2. Are these covenants similar?
   In a way, but it would be better to say that they have unity.

3. What are the three points Calvin makes here?
First, that the Jews aspired to more than earthly prosperity. Second, that the covenant they lived under was all of grace. And third, they knew Christ as Mediator.

[3]
Vantage from the Old Testament

1. According to the Bible, what were the Old Testament saints looking forward to?
To Christ and to the gospel.

2. What was the Old Testament particularly concerned with?
The future life.

[4]
A Notable Saying

1. What notable saying of the Lord does Calvin use in this discussion?
That Abraham rejoiced to see Christ's day (Jn. 8:56).

2. In passing, what does Calvin call the Lord's mother?
"The blessed Virgin."

[5]
Similar Signs

1. Does Calvin contrast the Jews in the wilderness with the Corinthians?
No, he compares them, showing their similarities.

2. If the Jews' baptism into Moses was carnal only, would Paul's argument have worked?
No, because Paul meant to disabuse Christians from thinking that they were superior to the Jews through the privilege of baptism.

[6]
Manna for Hunger Only

1. Does Calvin believe that manna was sacramental food?
Yes, he does.

2. How does he answer the objection from John 6:49, 54?
By explaining that Jesus was answering the Jews from the framework of their misunderstanding.

[7]

They Had the Word

1. In arguing for the spiritual benefits enjoyed by the Old Testament saints, what does Calvin point to in this section as their possession?
To their possession of the word, which has "such life energy" in it that anyone who possesses it possesses life.

[8]

God as Their God

1. What else did they possess?
God was their God, as the Lord promises them throughout the Old Testament. And how could they have Him and not have spiritual life?

[9]

A Third Argument

1. What is Calvin's next argument for the spiritual blessedness of the Old Testament saints?
God's promise to bless them in subsequent generations, which would come to fulfillment long after their deaths.

[10]

Earthly Trials

1. What is another reason for saying that they were not enjoying all the heaven they were going to get here on earth?
The fact that many of them went through extraordinary trials here on earth, just as we do.

[11]

The Trials of Abraham

1. Who was a preeminent example of this?
Abraham, who lived what Calvin describes as a "calamitous life." If all Abraham's blessings were to be enjoyed in this life, Calvin argues, something was seriously skewed.

[12]

The Trials of Isaac and Jacob

1. Did Isaac live as troubled a life as Abraham?
   No, but he still had a rough go. Calvin cites a number of examples.
2. What about Jacob?
   His earthly life was filled with various forms of grief, and he testified at the end of it that his life had been "short and evil."
3. What are the implications of this?
   Either that God's promises failed them, or that His promises were not directed at this life.

[13]

Looking to the Promises

1. What Scripture settles the issue?
   Hebrews 11:9–10, 13–16.

2. What would the patriarchs have been if God had promised them earthly blessing which they did not receive?
   They would have been more stupid than blocks of wood.

[14]

Open Expression

1. Did they ever express this hope openly?
   Yes. For example, Genesis 49:18.

[15–16]

David, Proclaimer of This Hope

1. What does David habitually call believers back to?
   To the fact that their happiness reposes elsewhere.
2. And what does he allude to throughout the Psalms?
   That the prosperity of believers is not to be grasped without reference to a manifestation of heavenly glory.

[17]

The Hope of the Godly

1. How often did Calvin believe that promises of blessedness were ful-filled in this life for Old Testament saints?
   Rarely or never.

2. Did this cause these saints to despair of the fulfillment?
No. They looked for the fulfillment in the next life.

[18]
The Flip Side

1. Did the wicked ever receive "blessings" in this life?
Yes, and it was a cause of temporary consternation. But the godly took refuge in considering their final end.

[19]
Job

1. Did Job expect a future life?
Yes (Job 19:25–27).

2. Was this an esoteric insight for just him?
No. Calvin denies that this was "secret wisdom" for just a few.

[20]
Progressive Revelation

1. If for Calvin the doctrine of the resurrection was clear in the earlier portions of the Old Testament, what happened later?
It became progressively clearer, as with a sunrise.

[21]
Dry Bones

1. How does Calvin interpret the valley of dry bones?
As a promise of restoration from exile which brought a promise of restoration in the afterlife.

[22]
Other Prophets

1. Which two prophets does Calvin cite here to reinforce this point?
Isaiah and Daniel.

[23]
Summary

1. What was the first of Calvin's two remaining points?
That the Old Testament saints had Christ as pledge of their covenant.

2. The second?
   That they put in Him all their future hopes.

3. So what doctrine falls to the ground?
   The notion that God had promised the Jews nothing but a full belly.

—————— CHAPTER ELEVEN ——————

[1]

Differences between the Testaments

1. How many differences are there between the Old and New Testaments?
   Depending on how you count, Calvin says, four or five.

2. What is the first of these differences?
   Calvin says that in the earthly possession which the Old Testament saints enjoyed, they had a teaching aid to help them see their future inheritance.

3. How did this differ from what Calvin's opponents said?
   They said that the Old Testament saints had earthly benefits only, which provided us with figures of our future inheritance, not theirs.

[2]

Childhood

1. Calvin reapplies an image that Paul used in Galatians. What is that image?
   The figure of Israel, the people of God, in their childhood. Now, in Christ, we, the Church, have come to maturity.

[3]

Benefits and Punishments as Types

1. What did Calvin believe about benefits and punishments in the Old Testament era?
   He believed that they were more "conspicuous."

2. What purpose did that serve?
   They were functioning as types and symbols of the spiritual blessings and punishments to come.

[4]
The Second Difference

1. What was the second difference between the two testaments?
    The Old Testament represented the substance in a figure; the New in reality.

2. What is the fulfillment of those figures?
    The fulfillment, when all is "finally confirmed and ratified," is Christ.

3. When did the covenant become new and eternal?
    Only after it was consecrated and established by the blood of Christ.

[5]
Childhood

1. Was the truth understood clearly and distinctly in the time of the Old Testament?
    No, Calvin says. It was understood, but there was "no great and shining revelation."

2. What did the Law and the Prophets point to, then?
    They gave a foretaste of the coming wisdom and "pointed to it twinkling afar off."

[6]
Great Men of Faith

1. Is this view consistent with understanding that few Christians if any measure up to Abraham's faith?
    No, it has nothing to do with how much grace was given to a few, but rather what the ordinary dispensation of grace was for His people.

[7]
Literal and Spiritual

1. According to Calvin, what is the third difference between the testaments?
    The Old Testament is literal, while the New is spiritual.

2. What does Calvin mean by those particular words?
    For example, the difference between the Ten Commandments being carved into stone (Old Testament) and carved into human hearts (New Testament).

[8]

The Difference in Detail

1. Why is the New Testament spiritual?
   Because it is engraved spiritually on men's hearts.

2. What is the final contrast between the testaments?
   The final contrast is to be referred to the status of the ceremonial laws.

3. What is the difference between the moral law and the ceremonial law in the Old Testament?
   The moral law was weak through the weakness of the people. The ceremonies had the cause of weakness in themselves.

[9]

Bondage and Freedom

1. What is the fourth contrast between the testaments?
   The Old Testament is one of "bondage," while the New is one of "freedom."

2. How then were Old Testament saints saved?
   They were saved as a fruit of the New Testament, working backward in time.

3. Nevertheless, what did these true saints of the Old Testament still have to do?
   They still had to offer sacrifices and observe the ceremonies.

[10]

Aspiring to Christ

1. How did the holy patriarchs live under the Old Covenant?
   Not as to remain there, but rather to aspire to the New.

[11]

All Nations

1. What is the fifth difference, which may be added?
   According to Calvin, the Lord confined His covenant of grace to one nation (Old Testament), until the advent of Christ (New Testament).

[12]

Calling of the Gentiles

1. What is therefore a "notable mark" of the excellence of the New Testament?
The calling and inclusion of the Gentiles.

2. Had the Old Testament foretold this?
Yes, but men were still surprised by it.

[13]

Is God Inconsistent Then?

1. Why did God change His manner of administration?
Because the circumstances were different. A farmer does different things at different times of year. This does not make him inconsistent.

[14]

A Basic Assumption

1. What is Calvin's basic assumption about all God's dealings with man?
That God does everything wisely and justly.

2. Is God doing all this for His own sake?
No, He is taking our condition and situation into account.

——— CHAPTER TWELVE ———

[1]

Bridge the Gulf

1. What was of the greatest importance?
That the Mediator be both true God and true man.

2. Where did this necessity come from?
From the heavenly decree.

3. Why did God have to descend to us?
Because it was not possible for us to ascend to Him.

[2]
Children of Men

1. What were the children of men to become?
   Children of God.

2. The heirs of Gehenna were to become what?
   Heirs of the heavenly kingdom.

3. Christ took our nature upon Him ungrudgingly in order to do what?
   Impart to us what was His.

[3]
Conquest of Death

1. The Incarnation was necessary how?
   *As God alone He could not feel death, and as man alone He could
   not conquer it.*

[4]
A Necessary Incarnation

1. What "speculation" does Calvin address next?
   *The view that Christ would have become a man even if Adam had
   not sinned.*

2. What does Calvin think of those who "leap over these bounds"?
   He believes it is the indulging of foolish curiosity.

[5]
Whose Mistake Is It?

1. Who is Calvin addressing in this section?
   The Protestant theologian Osiander.

2. Does Calvin believe that Adam's fall precedes God's decree in time?
   No. But it reveals what God determined before all ages.

[6]
Osiander's Doctrine

1. What is the basis of Osiander's teaching?
   *He holds that man is made in God's image because he was made
   after the pattern of the Messiah to come.*

[7]
Calvin's Reply

1. What is Calvin's reply concerning Christ's "pride of place"?
   He says that Scripture does not hesitate to describe Christ as a descendant of Adam. Not only so, but also as the second Adam.

2. Does Calvin believe that Christ could have been "Head" of the human race without the Incarnation?
   Yes. He is Head over the angels, and He never became one of them.

—— CHAPTER THIRTEEN ——

[1]
True Manhood

1. In this part of the *Institutes,* Calvin is answering three groups. Who are they?
   There were two ancient groups, the Marcionites and the Manichees. The group contemporary with Calvin was the Mennonites, led by Menno Simons. Modern Mennonites have not followed their founder's heresy at this point.

2. What were the two options suggested by these groups for the "body of Christ"?
   One suggested a phastasm, while the other proposed Christ had a heavenly body.

[2]
Emptied Himself

1. What does Calvin say Paul is not doing in Philippians 2:5–7?
   Paul is not teaching what Christ was, but rather how He conducted Himself.

2. What is the basic approach to answering these heresies?
   To simply quote the Bible in passage after passage, such as the one that simply says, "Christ shared in flesh and blood" (Heb. 2:14).

[3]

Christ and the Virgin Mary

1. According to Calvin, the genealogy in Matthew was whose?
   Joseph's.

2. Although the male line is the basis for reckoning in the political order, does this exclude women?
   No, Calvin says. Women must share in the act of generation.

3. What does Calvin argue concerning Mary engendering Christ from her seed?
   That Christ was begotten of Mary the same way that Isaac was begotten of Abraham.

[4]

True Man and Sinless

1. When the Word in His immeasurable essence was united with the nature of man into one person, did He leave heaven?
   No. He became one man; He was not confined to one man.

—— CHAPTER FOURTEEN ——

[1]

Two Natures

1. What two things must we not attribute to the two natures of Christ?
   That the Word "turned into" flesh or was "confusedly mingled" with it.

2. How then did the Son of God become the Son of Man?
   Not by confusion of substance, but by unity of person.

3. What illustration of this does Calvin use?
   The illustration of a body and soul.

[2]

Divinity and Humanity

1. How do we know that this doctrine was not "humanly devised"?
   Because of the many passages of Scripture that address it.

2. Can we ever speak of the attributes of one nature in terms of the other?

Yes, but only "improperly" and not strictly. We do this because of the unity of the person—as when God laid down His life for us (1 Jn. 3:16).

[3]
The Mediator

1. When we speak of the office of Mediator, which way do we speak?
We do not speak solely of the divine nature or of the human.

[4]
Two Natures

1. Those who stumble over the question of Christ's two natures do not consider what?
They don't consider Christ's person, in which He was manifested as God and man, and they do not consider the office of Mediator.

2. What does it mean when Christ calls His body a temple?
He did this because His divinity, as distinct from His body, dwelt there.

[5]
Hypostatic Union

1. How does Calvin define the hypostatic union?
As one person out of two natures.

[6–8]
Son of God, Son of Man

1. What did Servetus teach about this?
That Christ was not Son of God before the Incarnation.

2. Does Calvin struggle in answering the arguments of Servetus?
Not at all—"Servetus' other slander also gives us no more embarrassment."

3. What is Calvin's summary of Servetus' position?
That "the Son of God was from the beginning an idea, and even then was preordained to be the man who would become the essential image of God."

CHAPTER FIFTEEN

[1]

Three-Fold Office

1. According to Calvin, the office assigned to Christ consisted of what three parts?
   Prophet, priest, and king.

2. Is it enough to acknowledge the right names of these offices?
   No. The papists use them too, but "coldly and rather ineffectually."

[2]

The Prophet

1. Which of the offices does the title Christ apply to?
   All of them, because under the law, prophets were anointed with oil, and not just kings and priests.

2. Is the prophetic office extended to the Church?
   Yes, by virtue of the anointing being diffused from the Head to the members.

3. What should be known outside Christ?
   Nothing is worth knowing outside Him.

4. What is it not lawful to go beyond?
   The simplicity of the gospel.

[3]

The King

1. What is the nature of Christ's kingship?
   It is spiritual in nature.

2. What basic responsibility of a king does Calvin begin with?
   The responsibility of a king to protect his people.

[4]

The King of Blessing

1. How must we fight throughout our lives?
   Under the cross.

2. Where does Calvin locate our happiness?
   In the heavenly life.

3. In the midst of our trials here, what must we be content with?
That our King will never leave us destitute.

[5]

The Anointing Oil

1. What was the oil of gladness that anointed Christ?
The spirit of wisdom and understanding.

2. If Christ's kingdom does not lie in earthly pleasures or pomp, what does it lie in?
The Holy Spirit.

3. What can we not have one drop of apart from the Spirit?
Not one drop of vigor.

[6]

The Priestly Office

1. As priest, what does Christ do for us forever?
He is an everlasting intercessor.

2. In this new and different order, what two roles did Christ play?
He was both priest and sacrifice, the one offering and the one offered.

———— CHAPTER SIXTEEN ————

[1]

The Redeemer

1. Where did the name "Jesus" come from?
It was brought from heaven by an angel.

2. What happens if we turn away from Christ, however slightly?
Our salvation, which is in Him alone, begins to vanish.

[2]

What We Must First Grasp

1. What must happen before we can accept God's gift of life with the gratitude we owe?
Our minds must be struck and overwhelmed by the fear of God's wrath.

[3]

Loving the Unlovely

1. Does God love us before our salvation?
   Yes. Despite our corruptions He still finds something to love.

2. Can He just receive us that way?
   No. While we are still sinners, He cannot receive us completely. An atonement is necessary.

[4]

Love First

1. According to Calvin, did God love us before we were reconciled to Him?
   Yes. His love motivated the provision of the atonement and did not follow after it.

2. Which church father does he cite in agreement with this?
   Augustine.

[5]

Christ's Active Obedience

1. How did Christ accomplish salvation for us?
   By the whole course of His obedience.

2. We are freed from the curse of the law by what?
   By the whole life of Christ.

3. What passage in Galatians does Calvin claim as support for this?
   Galatians 4:4–5.

4. According to Calvin, was the means by which Christ died important?
   Yes—He needed to be tried as a criminal and die as a convicted criminal.

[6]

The Cross

1. What happened to the curse that was on us?
   It was transferred to Christ on the cross.

2. What exchange did the Son of God make, even though He was utterly clean of all fault?
   He took on Himself the shame of our iniquities, and He clothed us with His purity.

3. Christ cleansed our filth by what means?
   By being covered with them by transferred imputation.

4. Even though it was full of shame, what was the cross changed into?
   A triumphal chariot.

[7]

The Death of Jesus

1. What two things did the death of Jesus accomplish?
   Our freedom from death (now conquered), and our freedom from the old man.

[8]

Descent into Hell

1. Does Calvin believe that the descent into hell belongs in the Creed?
   Yes, he does, although he does grant that it was a late addition.

[9]

A Traditional View Rejected

1. What traditional view does Calvin reject with regard to this article?
   He rejects the idea that Christ descended into the nether world, into Hades.

[10]

Soul Struggles

1. If Calvin rejects the idea that Christ descended into the nether world, how does he take the phrase from the Creed?
   He interprets it as referring to the soul agonies that Christ suffered while on the cross.

2. Does the compiler of these study questions agree with this?
   Nope.

[11]

Scripture Proof

1. How does Calvin undertake to prove this view?
   By showing that the Bible teaches that Christ did in fact go through soul agonies on the cross, which He did.

[12]

Answering the Critics

1. How does Calvin answer his critics on this point?
   By engaging with them on the question of whether or not Christ did suffer soul agonies, and he makes a strong case.

[13]

The Resurrection

1. What must faith do in order to attain its full strength?
   It must leap over the cross, death, and burial of Jesus and come to the resurrection.

2. What is the summary of the effects of the death and resurrection respectively?
   Sin was taken away by His death, and righteousness was brought by His resurrection.

3. What should we understand in Scripture when the benefits of His death or resurrection are spoken of singly?
   We should understand the presence of the other by synecdoche.

[14]

The Ascension

1. What did Christ's ascension do for His relation to all things?
   It enabled Him to fill all things, as Paul teaches in Ephesians.

2. The ascension of Christ's body did what to His power and energy?
   The ascension of Christ's body diffused and spread His power and energy beyond all the bounds of heaven and earth.

[15]

The Right Hand

1. What is the central meaning of Christ's position at the right hand of God the Father?
   The central meaning is rule and authority.

[16]

What the Ascension Did for Us

1. What did Jesus do for us by means of His ascent into heaven?
   He opened the way for us.

2. Do we look forward to heaven as with a "bare hope"?
No, but rather to our Head in whom we already possess it.

[17]

Kingdom Come

1. Despite His present power, where is Christ's kingdom now?
It is hidden in the earth, under the lowness of the flesh.

2. Will any escape His judgment when He returns?
No one. He will judge the living and the dead.

[18]

Our Judge and Redeemer

1. Who will share with Him in the work of judging?
Some of those who are to be judged.

2. What can a head not do?
A head cannot scatter its own members.

3. What does the Son do with the judgment He has been given?
He cares for our consciences.

[19]

In Every Clause

1. What do we find in every clause of the Creed?
We find Christ in every clause.

———— CHAPTER SEVENTEEN ————

[1]

Grace and Merit

1. When discussing the merit of Christ, what must we remember lies behind it?
The grace of God.

2. Did "that man," according to Augustine, deserve to be the only begotten Son of God?
No. It was entirely the grace of God.

[2]
Love and Hate

1. What was God's ineffable demeanor toward us?
   He loved us and was angry with us at the same time.

[3]
Christ's Obedience

1. What did Christ accomplish by His obedience?
   He truly acquired and merited grace for us with His Father.

[4]
The Substitution

1. What power did Christ's sacrifice have?
   The power of expiating, appeasing, and making satisfaction.

[5]
The Price of Redemption

1. What is the definition of redemption in Christ's blood?
   It is forgiveness of sins (Col. 1:14).

[6]
Merit Not for Himself

1. Did Christ merit anything for Himself?
   No. Calvin dismisses it as a stupid question.

BOOK THREE

THE WAY IN WHICH WE RECEIVE THE GRACE OF CHRIST

What benefits come to us from it, and what effects follow

CHAPTER ONE

[1]

The Spirit Bond

1. What has to happen before all Christ's benefits become ours?
   We have to grow up into one body with Him.
2. What is the bond that unites us to Christ?
   The Holy Spirit.

[2]

The Universal Spirit

1. What does the Spirit do for all living creatures?
   He quickens and nourishes them in what we call their natural life.
2. But what does He do for the believers?
   He is also the root and seed of heavenly life in us.
3. Does the Spirit belong to the Father or the Son?
   Both. He is sometimes called the Spirit of the Father, sometimes the Spirit of the Son.

[3]

Titles of the Spirit

1. What are some of the titles or names given to the Spirit that Calvin records here?
   Spirit of adoption, guarantee and seal, life, water, oil, fire, and more.

[4]
The Spirit's Work

1. What is the principal work of the Holy Spirit?
   Faith is the principal work of the Holy Spirit.

—————— CHAPTER TWO ——————

[1]
Faith in Christ

1. Is it hard for us to keep the law?
   Not only hard, but beyond our strength entirely.
2. What inadequate notion of faith does Calvin address first?
   Nothing deeper than a common assent to the gospel history.
3. What two things must we know?
   Our destination and the way to it.
4. How does Christ the God/man help us in this?
   As God He is the destination; as man He is the way.

[2]
Knowledge and Faith

1. What fiction does Calvin reject?
   The idea of implicit faith, faith in whatever the church teaches.

[3]
Implicit Faith False

1. Does Calvin believe that ignorance should be tempered by humility?
   Yes, but it would be absurd to call this faith.
2. What does Scripture regularly teach about this?
   That understanding is joined with faith.

[4]
There Is Such a Thing

1. Does Calvin believe that there is such a thing as implicit faith?
   Yes, but only to the extent that certain things are hidden from us.

[5]
Prefaith

1. Is there something else that we may call implicit faith?
   Yes. There is a demeanor that is actually preparation for faith. It is a good thing, but it is not yet faith.

2. Are there believers who are not yet believers in an exact sense?
   Yes. They are in the process of being drawn in.

[6]
True Knowledge of Christ

1. How must we receive Christ?
   As He is offered by the Father, that is, clothed in the gospel.

2. How does Paul define faith?
   As the obedience that is given to the gospel.

[7]
How Faith Arises

1. Does the word of God automatically build faith?
   No. Some statements from God will do nothing but shake our faith.

2. Should we decide that God is well disposed toward us?
   Not unless He gives us a witness of Himself.

[8]
Formed and Unformed Faith

1. What does Calvin think of the scholastic distinction between formed and unformed faith?
   He calls it worthless.

2. How does the assent of faith work?
   It comes more from the heart than from the brain and is called the obedience of faith.

3. What can faith not be separated from?
   A devout disposition.

[9]
Not All Faith the Same

1. How does Calvin answer the proof from 1 Corinthians 13 that argues that if faith is described as being without love, there must be something like unformed faith?

Calvin shows that "faith" in that passage is talking about miraculous powers.

2. What mistake is made by Calvin's adversaries here?

They argue as though the definition of a word must be the same everywhere in Scripture.

[10]
The Faith of Simon Magus

1. What common explanation of Simon Magus' behavior does Calvin reject?

He rejects the idea that Simon Magus pretended with words to have a faith he did not actually have in his heart.

2. What kind of faith did he have then?

He had a temporary faith, one that resembles the real thing in many ways.

3. What is the human heart like, such that it makes self-deception possible?

The heart has "so many crannies where vanity hides, so many holes where falsehood lurks" and is "decked out with deceiving hypocrisies." It often "dupes itself."

[11]
The Faith of the Reprobate

1. What is hard to some?

The idea that the reprobate can have faith.

2. Yet what do the reprobate sometimes experience?

A feeling that is almost the same as that experienced by the elect.

3. What does Calvin call the effecting of this kind of transitory faith?

He calls it the "lower working of the Spirit." Nothing prevents God from doing a temporary work in some.

[12]

Common Faith

1. In what way are the reprobate in this sense compared to a tree?
   They are like a tree not planted deep enough, a tree that may for a time put forth blossoms and leaves, and even fruit. But they don't have what Calvin calls living roots.

2. What is common faith?
   The faith that both the elect and reprobate have—there is great likeness and affinity between them. And yet they differ because one is transitory and the other is living and permanent.

[13]

Different Uses of the Word "Faith"

1. What must we understand about the meaning of the word "faith"?
   That the meaning of the word is ambiguous.

2. Does the Bible use the word in ways that allow the reprobate to have "faith"?
   Yes. Some "fall from faith" for example (1 Tim. 6:20–21).

[14]

Higher Faith

1. Does faith comprehend what it knows?
   No. What our mind embraces by faith is in every way infinite.

[15]

Certainty by Faith

1. According to Calvin, what does genuine faith require?
   It requires full and fixed certainty.

2. What is God's intention with regard to us?
   To uproot perverse doubts from our hearts.

[16]

Owning It

1. Is it enough to believe that God is merciful to many?
   No. True faith believes that God is "merciful to me."

2. What does the man who "hopes well" in the Lord do?
   He confidently glories in his heavenly inheritance.

[17]

Faith That Struggles

1. If faith is essentially certain, then what must we explain in the believer's experience?
   The fact that believers are in "perpetual conflict with their own unbelief."

2. Who does Calvin use as a prime example of this?
   David, a man of faith, describes his unsettled emotional condition in numerous Psalms.

[18]

The Believer's Conflict

1. How does this variation arise within us?
   It arises because of the imperfection of faith.

2. What does this imperfect faith do?
   Even though imperfect, it ultimately triumphs.

[19]

Weak Faith Is Real Faith

1. What illustration of weak but real faith does Calvin use?
   A prisoner in a dungeon cannot see the full light of the sun, but only a slanting ray of light. Nevertheless he does see the sun.

[20]

Both Weak and Strong

1. In this life, what must we put up with?
   The fact that faith and unbelief get jumbled up together.

[21]

Shielded by the Word

1. Although believers have to deal with unbelief, where does it come from?
   Unbelief does not arise from within, but assails believers from without.

2. What illustration of shaken faith does Calvin give?
   It is like a soldier forced to give way for a moment, and so he moves his foot, giving ground a little. But he fights on.

[22]

Right Fear

1. What are the two kinds of fear?
   One diminishes assurance of faith, while the right kind firmly establishes it.

2. What might happen among the Gentiles that had happened among the Jews?
   Some covenant members might arise without true faith and abuse God's generosity.

[23]

The Right Kind of Constant Fear

1. What kind of man does Solomon pronounce a blessing on?
   The man who is always afraid in his own heart, that is, a man constantly cautious about his possible sin.

[24]

Union with Christ

1. What does Calvin call those who believe that we have assurance so long as we look to Christ (over there)?
   He calls them half-papists.

2. What is the basis for our assurance in Christ?
   The fact that He has joined Himself to us. We have assurance because we have been made members with Him.

[25]

An Extensive Quotation

1. What medieval father does Calvin quote extensively and with approval on this subject of faith?
   Bernard of Clairvaux.

[26]

Fear and Honor

1. What do our duties of fear and honor relate to?
   Honor is the obedience we render to God as Father, and fear is the service that is offered to Him as Lord.

[27]

True and False Fear

1. What distinguishes childlike and servile fear?
   Believers fear offending God, while unbelievers only fear offending God because of what He can do to them.

[28]

What God Promises

1. Does God guarantee believers earthly prosperity?
   No, according to Calvin.

2. What does He promise then?
   However many things fail us, God will never fail us.

[29]

The Basic Foundation

1. What is the foundation of faith?
   The freely given promise of God.

[30]

Faith Dependent

1. What must a man attain to in the first place to have faith?
   The freely given promise.

2. What must also happen in order for this faith to reconcile us to God?
   It must join us to Christ.

[31]

The Word Needed

1. Can faith latch on to nothing?
   No. Faith needs to be according to the word.

2. What must God do to bring about faith?
   He must illumine the word by the testimony of His grace.

[32]

Fulfilled in Christ

1. What is the testimony of God's love toward us?
   Any promise whatever.

2. Did the ancient Jews know of Christ?
   Obscurely, but yes.

[33]
Real Faith

1. How do the Schoolmen go completely astray on the question of faith?
   By considering assent to knowledge as faith, leaving out confidence and assurance of heart.

[34]
The Spirit's Leading

1. Can we find our way unless someone leads us?
   No. The Spirit must bring us to the promises of Christ.

2. What does Calvin compare the word to?
   He compares it to the sun which, when it shines on a blind man, does not bring light.

[35]
Unfit for Belief

1. What does our corruption of nature do to our capacity for faith?
   It renders us unfit to believe.

2. Can man initiate faith?
   No.

3. What then is necessary for belief?
   The Spirit of faith must be given.

[36]
Top of the Brain

1. What is not true faith?
   When the word flits about in the top of the brain instead of taking root in the heart.

2. What is greater than the mind's blindness?
   The heart's distrust.

[37]

Shaken, Not Broken

1. Can true faith be shaken?

Yes, according to Calvin's earlier argument. But it cannot be toppled.

[38]

The Schoolmen Again

1. According to the Schoolmen, how do we discern the grace of God toward us?

By moral conjecture. That is, when men determine that they are not unworthy of it.

2. What does Calvin say faith should correspond to?

To a simple and free promise.

[39]

Christian Joy

1. Is it a small error the Schoolmen have fallen into?

No. They trip over the first rudiments of the Christian faith.

2. Do the Schoolmen deny that we have the Spirit?

No, but they think it modest and humble to be unsure of it.

3. What is to charge with arrogance those Christians who dare to glory in the presence of the Holy Spirit?

It is miserable blindness.

[40]

Is Our Future Unknown?

1. What other argument against assurance is brought?

The argument that knowledge of our final perseverance remains in suspense.

2. Did Paul say what he did in Romans 8:38–39 by special revelation in his own case?

No, Paul is talking about what all believers share in common.

3. What does doubt about our future reveal instead of modesty?

Ingratitude.

[41]

The Substance of Faith

1. What translation of *hypostasis* in Hebrews 11:1 does Calvin prefer?
   He prefers "substance," but he can live with "confidence."

2. What teaching of the Schoolmen does Calvin dismiss as mere madness?
   The idea that love is prior to faith and hope.

3. What three things does Bernard teach about the glory of the pious?
   That there is no forgiveness apart from mercy, that we can do no good works unless God gives it, and that we cannot merit eternal life by any works unless they are also given.

4. Does Calvin approve of this?
   Strongly.

[42]

Faith and Hope

1. What is the foundation of hope?
   Faith.

2. How does faith look forward to our future blessedness?
   In hope.

[43]

The Foundation

1. What common foundation do faith and hope share?
   The mercy of God.

———————— CHAPTER THREE ————————

[1]

Repentance Born of Faith

1. According to Calvin, does true repentance follow faith or precede it?
   It follows faith, arising from it.

[2]

Foundation in the Gospel

1. How does he deal with the objection that in Scripture, the command to repent comes first?

He says that people are superstitiously clinging to the joining of syllables without considering the meaning that ties those words together.

[3]

Two Aspects of Repentance

1. What two aspects of repentance does Calvin discuss?

Mortification and vivification.

2. How does Calvin define them?

Mortification is contrition—hatred and loathing for the sin. Calvin defines vivification as the positive desire to live a holy and devout life.

[4]

Two Kinds of Repentance

1. What are the two kinds of repentance?

Repentance of the law and repentance of the gospel.

2. Unless it comes to the latter, what does repentance of the law accomplish?

It serves as an entryway to hell.

[5]

Faith and Repentance

1. What is the relationship of faith and repentance?

They can be distinguished, but not separated.

2. What does Calvin draw from the Hebrew and Greek meanings of their words for repentance?

He derives the sense of conversion from the Hebrew, and a change of mind or intention from the Greek.

[6]

Repentance Defined

1. What is the first of three heads in Calvin's understanding of repentance?

He defines it as a turning of the life to God, inner life included.

[7]

Earnest Fear

1. What is the second of these three heads?
   An earnest fear of God, knowing that He will bring everything into judgment.

[8]

Mortification and Vivification

1. What simple expression of mortification and vivification is used by the prophets?
   Turn from evil and do good.

2. Is mortification easy?
   No. The word itself indicates how difficult it is to forget our previous nature.

[9]

Lifelong Regeneration

1. How does Calvin sum up his understanding of repentance?
   He defines it as regeneration.

2. Does this regeneration take place at one moment in time?
   No. It occurs throughout the course of our lives.

3. How does Calvin interpret the image of God?
   As true holiness and righteousness.

[10]

Believers Still Sinners

1. In this life, do we receive entire freedom from sin?
   No. We do not receive "full possession of freedom."

2. What remains within every believer?
   A "smoldering cinder of evil."

3. Where does Calvin differ with Augustine on this point?
   Calvin calls this smoldering ember sin proper, while Augustine identifies it as a corrupt weakness.

[11]

Remaining, Not Reigning

1. What is the believer's relation to sin?
   Sin remains within him, but it is not to reign in him.

2. Do we have to worry about our salvation because of this remaining sin?
   No. Through the mercy of God we are freed from this guilt.

[12]

Natural Corruption

1. Did God create these corruptions?
   No. All that God created was good. Sin was our contribution.

[13]

Augustine's Witness

1. Does Calvin think there is a substantive difference between himself and Augustine on this?
   No. He thinks that Augustine was too wary about using the word "sin" because of his controversy with the Pelagians, but Calvin shows that Augustine knew that our remaining weaknesses are in fact sinful.

[14]

Sinless Perfection

1. According to Calvin, what is the cause of certain Anabaptists claiming an antinomian perfection?
   They are blinded by the madness of lusts and have put off common sense.

2. What does the Spirit not do in leading us?
   He is not giddy, and He does not run headlong through right and wrong.

[15]

True Repentance

1. How many aspects of repentance does Paul outline in 2 Corinthians 7:11?
   Seven—earnestness, excuse, indignation, fear, longing, zeal, and avenging.

2. In repentance, what must we exercise?
   Restraint, lest sorrow engulf us.

[16]

The Measure

1. In order to keep the signs of repentance sure, what must a man measure his life by?
   By the standard of God's law.

2. What are the two dangers of "exercises" to aid repentance?
   They obscure internal repentance, and they tend to make the church severe when the church should be gentle.

[17]

Fasting

1. When fasting is necessary, what proviso does Calvin urge pastors to teach?
   That the people remember the principal point and rend their hearts, not their garments.

[18]

Open Confession

1. What is the difference between special repentance and ordinary repentance?
   Special repentance is only required of some, when open sin makes public repentance necessary. Ordinary repentance is heart repentance and is required of all, in that corruption of nature requires our attention throughout our lives.

[19]

Repentance and Forgiveness

1. Under what two headings is the whole gospel contained?
   Repentance and forgiveness of sins.

2. Where do these two things come from?
   They are the gift of God, and both are received by faith.

[20]

How Repentance Is Prior

1. Is repentance the *basis* for our receiving pardon?
   No. The Lord already determined to have pity on men, and He wanted them to know what direction to look. That is the reason we are called to repentance.

[21]

Free Gift

1. Why does Calvin believe that repentance is a gift of God?
   Because of Acts 11:18; 2 Corinthians 7:10; and 2 Timothy 2:25–26.
2. What does the efficacy of this gift depend on?
   On the Spirit of regeneration.
3. In passing, who does Calvin believe to be the author of Hebrews?
   Paul.

[22]

Unpardonable

1. Where does Calvin differ with Augustine on the unpardonable sin?
   He points out that it must be committed in the present life.
2. How does Calvin define the unpardonable sin?
   The sin is committed when one, with evil intention, resists the illumination of God, knowing it to be the illumination of God.
3. What is a brief way of summarizing this sin?
   Mixing knowledge with unbelief.

[23]

The Point of No Return

1. Is this a sin that a man can fall into accidentally one day?
   No. It is a complete turning away from God. It is apostasy of the whole man.

[24]

Too Hard

1. Is this teaching consistent with the tender mercies of God?
   Yes. The point is not that men who have done this seek forgiveness but are denied. Rather it is that because they have turned away from God, they never repent. They have passed the point of no return, and they do not attempt to return.

[25]
Temporal Repentance

1. Does God ever show mercy short of eternal mercy?
Yes. God shows mercy that is commensurate with the repentance. Temporal repentance can result in a temporal "stay of judgment." Calvin cites the examples of Ahab and Esau.

———— CHAPTER FOUR ————

[1]
Penance

1. What are the three elements of repentance, according to the Scholastics?
Contrition, confession, and satisfaction.

2. And according to Calvin, how do they heal all the bitterness?
With a light sprinkling of ceremonies.

[2]
Not a Small Thing

1. Why does Calvin say that this is not a dispute "over the shadow of an ass"?
Because it revolves around forgiveness of sin.

[3]
Desperation

1. When someone follows the Scholastics in this, what are the two possible responses?
Desperation on the one hand, and pretended rather than true sorrow on the other.

[4]
The Ten Lepers

1. How does Calvin respond to the Scholastics' allegorical argument from the ten lepers?
By pointing to Christ. The "whole right and honor of the priesthood has . . . been transferred to Him."

2. And how does Calvin explain why Christ sent the lepers to the priests?
In order to make the Jews witnesses of Christ's miraculous power.

[5]
Allegory

1. What does Calvin say about allegorical interpretation and dogma?
He says that allegories are of no great value in confirming any dogma.

[6]
Confession

1. How does Calvin handle the argument for confession from the baptism of John the Baptist?
By saying that it was a baptism of repentance, which made confession necessary given the nature of the case.

2. What about James' requirement that we confess our sins to one another (Jas. 5:16)?
Calvin points out that a priest is not involved—we do this for one another. The passage proves too much.

[7]
History of Auricular Confession

1. When was auricular confession made a matter of canon law?
At the time of Innocent III, twelve hundred years after the resurrection of Christ.

2. What other historical argument does Calvin use?
That it is not practiced in the east.

[8]
Chrysostom

1. What did Chrysostom teach on the subject of confession of sin?
According to Calvin, he repeatedly urged his parishioners to confess their sins privately to God.

[9]

Confession before God

1. What mistake in interpretation did the defenders of auricular confession make?
   They took passages that translated "to praise" as "to confess" and treated them as though they were talking about confession of sin.
2. Calvin then cites a number of passages to prove what?
   That we should confess our sins to the Lord.

[10]

Confession before Men?

1. If we have confessed to God, what are the two circumstances that would require confession to men?
   If the divine glory or our humiliation demands it.
2. What passage in the Old Testament urges public confession?
   Leviticus 16:21.

[11]

General Confession

1. When should people confess all together?
   When they have sinned all together.
2. What other circumstance should lead us to confess our sins corporately?
   Whenever there is war, pestilence, barrenness, or any other sort of calamity. These are all signs of our guilt.

[12]

Private Confession

1. Scripture approves two forms of private confession to others. What are they?
   When we confess for our own sake (Jas. 5:16), and when we confess for the sake of a brother whom we have offended.
2. What role do ministers have in this?
   They are to counsel those who need it and declare assurance of pardon.
3. To whom do we commend private confession?
   To those who know they have need of it.

[13]

More on Private Confession

1. What does Calvin ardently wish was observed everywhere?
   The sheep coming to the shepherd for the Sacred Supper "as often as they wish."

2. If this were observed, Calvin would desire two things to be avoided. What are they?
   Tyranny and superstition.

[14]

Power of the Keys

1. What are the three occasions, according to Calvin, when the power of the keys is to be used?
   When the whole church has offended, when one man has been disciplined by the church, and in private counsel.

2. What must we not "dream up" with regard to the power of the keys?
   Some power separate from the preaching of the gospel.

[15]

The Roman Doctrine

1. What Roman practice is Calvin opposing?
   The requirement that every Catholic make confession at least once a year, with all sins enumerated, and with the intent to confess.

[16]

Impossible

1. What does Calvin see as one problem with this?
   The enumeration of our sins for one day is impossible; how could we do it for a year?

[17]

Butchery

1. What does Calvin call this requirement?
   Butchery of souls.

2. How do Roman theologians categorize sins?
   Into arms, branches, twigs, and leaves, according to their formulas.

3. And what did they discover when they were done?
That they had put out to open sea, with no port or anchorage anywhere, and no refuge possible.

[18]
Pernicious Effects

1. Does Calvin agree that sins should be confessed singly?
Yes, but only as possible—and to God, not "some priestling."

2. What promise from the prophet Ezekiel does he quote?
"Whenever the sinner bewails his sins, I shall not recall all his iniquities" (Ezek. 18:21–22).

[19]
Wholesale Confession

1. What is the problem with the requirement that Catholics make confession once a year?
They "vomit them up at once" and are careless throughout the year in between confessions.

[20]
Power of the Keys

1. According to Calvin, what is necessary in order to hold the power of the keys?
"I deny that the power of they keys belongs to any persons who have not first received the Holy Spirit."

[21]
Deep Uncertainty

1. What is the central problem with auricular confession?
It can bring no assurance. The system is biased against assurance.

[22]
Protestant Absolution

1. Why is the Protestant practice free of "these absurdities"?
Because the Protestant minister makes his declaration conditionally. Each person hears according to their faith.

[23]

Discipline

1. Why do passages like Matthew 18:15–18 have nothing to do with auricular confession?

Because they relate to the discipline of the church and have nothing to do with secret sins.

[24]

Twin Errors

1. What are the twin errors that arise when the Roman doctrine is practiced?

Where people fear God, they fall into despair; where they do not, they become sluggish.

[25]

Satisfaction

1. What doctrine was Calvin countering here?

The idea that baptism washes all sins away, but sins committed after baptism must be dealt with in part by penance.

[26]

Fear and Honor

1. What do our duties of fear and honor relate to?

Honor is the obedience we render to God as Father, and fear is the service that is offered to Him as Lord.

[27]

Two Problems

1. What two things is Calvin concerned to press home in this section?

First, that we must be zealous for Christ's honor, and second, that assurance of pardon is something that should really assure the conscience, not torment it.

[28]

Venial and Mortal

1. What does Calvin do with the distinction between venial and mortal sin?

He rejects it, holding that all sin is mortal.

2. What objection does he dismiss?
That this means he must be saying that all sin is the same. But he does not hold to the equality of all sin—he holds that all unequal sins are mortal.

[29]
Forgiveness Is Full

1. What distinction does the Roman position attempt?
A distinction between the penalty for sin and the guilt of sin. They say God's mercy deals with the guilt, but that we must merit remission of the penalty.

2. How does Calvin respond?
What "flitting levity is this!" Forgiveness is forgiveness, all the way down.

[30]
Penalty and Guilt

1. What must a man attain to in the first place to have faith?
The freely given promise.

2. What must also happen in order for this faith to reconcile us to God?
It must join us to Christ.

[31]
Punishment and Discipline

1. What are the two kinds of judgment, according to Calvin?
They are a judgment of teaching and a judgment of vengeance.

2. What role does God have in each?
That of father and judge, respectively.

[32]
The Distinction

1. What is characteristic of the judgment of vengeance?
Correction and instruction are not in view, only justice.

2. What is the characteristic of the judgment of teaching?
We learn to receive the admonition and receive the correction.

3. What is the difference between how two classes of people receive these respective judgments?
The ungodly respond with fury, and the godly are suppliants for pardon.

[33]
Orientation

1. What is the difference between discipline and punishment with respect to time?
   Discipline is oriented to the future; punishment to the past.
2. When we as children of God are afflicted, what is it for?
   It is not a penalty to confound us; it is a chastisement to instruct us.

[34]
Not to Lose Heart

1. Why must believers be exhorted not to lose heart?
   Because the discipline, even though it is only discipline, can be severe.

[35]
David's Discipline

1. Why was David disciplined with various calamities?
   Because he was a beloved and faithful servant.

[36]
Love Covers

1. What is Solomon referring to when he says that love covers a multitude of sins?
   This is not before God, but among men.

[37]
The Sinful Woman

1. How does Calvin prove that the woman who was forgiven much because she loved much did not earn her forgiveness?
   By looking at Christ's illustration for it. The man who had been forgiven the debt of many denarii loved for that reason. He was not forgiven the debt because he loved.

[38–39]

The Church Fathers

1. What is Calvin's view of the church fathers on this subject?
He says that they were sound in the main. In places, they spoke poorly but were nowhere near as bad as the Schoolmen made them out to be.

—————— CHAPTER FIVE ——————

[1]

Indulgences

1. From which doctrine does the practice of granting indulgences flow?
From the doctrine of satisfaction.

2. Does Calvin want to argue with the men who advance these notions?
No, he would rather administer drugs for insanity.

[2]

Root and Fruit

1. What do many people see, and what do they miss?
They see the corrupt practices, but they do not see the root from which it all flows.

2. What do indulgences establish?
Another purchase price for the saints in the blood of the martyrs.

[3]

Fathers against Indulgences

1. What two fathers does Calvin cite against the practice?
Leo and Augustine.

2. According to this doctrine, does the merit of Christ mingle with the merit of the saints in the treasury of the church?
Yes, and according to Calvin, this makes Christ one of a throng, a "saintlet."

[4]

Filling Up Afflictions

1. What then does the apostle Paul mean in Colossians 1:24?
   Calvin shows that this does not refer to propitiation or redemption, but rather to the filling up of Christ's sufferings in His extended body, the Church.

[5]

Indulgences and the Unity of Redemption

1. What does the practice of offering indulgences do to the redemption of Christ?
   It divvies it up into pieces and destroys the unity of that redemption.

[6]

Purgatory

1. What destroys the notion of purgatory before it is even discussed?
   The biblical idea of satisfaction in Christ alone, which Calvin has already established. This is the "ax" that overturns the doctrine of purgatory.

2. Could the idea of purgatory be a trifle not worth discussing at all?
   Yes, but not if it is linked to the atonement. When expiation of sins is sought anywhere other than in the blood of Christ, the issue is very important.

[7–8]

History of Auricular Confession

1. What proofs of purgatory were offered from the gospels?
   For example, if a certain sin was not to be remitted in the age to come, does this not hint that others might be? Calvin dismisses this kind of argumentation as trifling.

2. What proofs are offered from Philippians and Revelation?
   The references there to the netherworld. But Calvin points out that they say nothing about human inhabitants suffering there for their sins.

3. How does he handle the proof from Maccabees?
   By rejecting that book from the canon, citing Augustine, Jerome, and Cyprian. He also points out in passing that Maccabees does not teach the existence of purgatory.

[9]

The Crucial Passage

1. What passage in Paul was considered by Calvin to be crucial to the purgatory debate?

First Corinthians 3:12–15. What fire could this be, they ask, but the fire of purgatory?

2. How does Calvin handle this passage?

The fire is the hour of the Holy Spirit's testing of each man's work.

3. And what class of men does this testing come upon?

Builders of the church who build on a lawful foundation with unsuitable materials.

[10]

The Fathers

1. Does Calvin acknowledge that many of the fathers went along with prayers for the dead?

Yes, he does. But he draws a distinction between the zealous heat his adversaries display for purgatory on the one hand, and the nervous coldness shown by the fathers on the other.

———— CHAPTER SIX ————

[1]

Christian Life

1. What is the object of regeneration?

That there be harmony between God's righteousness and our obedience.

2. What is one danger for those who heartily repent?

That they err in their zeal.

3. What is different between the teaching of the Holy Spirit and the teaching of moral philosophers?

The Spirit teaches without affectation.

[2]

Two Main Aspects

1. What are the two main aspects of scriptural instruction?
   One is the inculcation of a love for righteousness; the second is that bounds are set so that we don't wander aimlessly in a misguided zeal for righteousness.

2. What is the nature of our bond with God?
   It is holiness, but not because we come to Him by virtue of our holiness.

[3]

The Strongest Motive

1. What is the strongest motive to the Christian life?
   It is Christ Himself.

2. Why must we not disfigure ourselves with sin?
   Because we are engrafted into His body.

[4]

Spurious Christians

1. What group does Calvin upbraid in this section?
   Those who have nothing but the name and badge of Christ.

2. Who only has true intimacy with Christ?
   Those who have a right understanding of Christ from the word of the gospel.

[5]

No Perfectionism

1. Why does Calvin not withhold the name "Christian" from those who have not attained to an evangelical perfection?
   Because then there would be no Christians.

2. What should we not be discouraged by?
   Our slow progress. We should be able to see true progress in holiness without pretending we are already there.

CHAPTER SEVEN

[1]

Owned by Another

1. What is the central principle to remember in Christian living?
   That we are consecrated and dedicated to God; that we belong to Him.

2. To what must reason submit?
   Reason must subject itself to the Holy Spirit.

[2]

True Devotion

1. What does godly self-denial lead to?
   Devotion to the glory of God and loss of all craving for human glory.

2. What happens when virtue is pursued for its own sake?
   It leads to a puffed-up arrogance.

[3]

Self-Denial

1. According to Calvin, what three aspects of Christian living does Paul give to Titus?
   Soberness, righteousness, and godliness.

[4]

Right Toward Others

1. What relation does self-denial have to our fellow men and to God?
   It has regard partly to men, but chiefly to God.

2. What happens when we rush into self-love?
   We believe we have just cause to be proud of ourselves, despising all others in comparison.

3. What does each person find within his breast through self-flattery?
   A kind of kingdom which comes in conflict with others easily.

[5]

Helpfulness

1. What will keep you from accomplishing anything in this life?
   Failure to give up thoughts of self; failure to get out of yourself.

2. What makes up the lawful use of all benefits to others?
   A liberal and kindly sharing of those benefits.

3. What makes the acceptance of an enjoyment unlawful?
   Failure to consecrate that enjoyment to God in the first place.

[6]

Loving the Unworthy

1. Do our neighbors deserve to be loved by us?
   No, not if we judge by merit.

2. How then may we love them?
   By considering the image of God in them.

3. When faced with the duty of loving someone unworthy, what should
   we do?
   *We should treat that person as a placeholder for the Lord and ask
   what the Lord deserved from us. If the person has sinned against us,
   we should charge it to the Lord's account.*

[7]

True Sincerity

1. For Calvin, are loving actions sufficient?
   No, they must also proceed from a sincere feeling of love.

2. How can liberal actions be made reprehensible?
   With a proud countenance or even insolent words.

3. When we give to the downtrodden, what must we experience?
   We must identify with them, thinking of ourselves in that position.

[8]

Devotion to His Will

1. When we learn self-denial, what two things form in us?
   Fair-mindedness and tolerance.

2. Our fear of what is wonderful to contemplate?
   Poverty, lowly birth, and humble condition.

3. What must happen for true prosperity to occur?
   God must bless.

[9]

God's Blessing Alone

1. When we look for divine blessing on our labors, what is bridled in us?
   The desire to grow rich or ambitiously pant after honors.

2. If we rest in God, what outcomes will we be content in?
   We will be content in either blessing or want.

[10]

Bearing Adversity

1. What part of our lives must we entrust to God?
   Every part. God is master over all of it.

2. If we are confident in this, what will we do in adversity?
   We will remain firm in our trust.

3. This firm resolve in adversity must not be confused with what pagan view?
   The stoic resolve not to complain against fortune since fortune is blind.

4. How does God structure our lives?
   With a most orderly justice.

———— CHAPTER EIGHT ————

[1]

Bearing the Cross

1. If we have been adopted by the Lord, what should we be prepared for?
   A life that is hard, toilsome, and unquiet, crammed with various kinds of evil.

2. Was the Lord exempt from this in His life?
   No, He had the same kind of troubles as He lived His life as a perfect example.

[2]

Leading Us to Trust

1. Why does God subject us to this kind of thing?
   So that our feebleness might be revealed to us. When in prosperity, we draw the wrong conclusions entirely.

[3]
Learning Endurance

1. What does the cross strike at?
   Our perilous confidence in the flesh.
2. Apart from trials given by God, could we learn these things?
   No, endurance is quite unattainable by our own efforts.

[4]
The Point of Trials

1. What is the testing function of trials?
   They reveal the difference between true faith and spurious faith.

[5]
Trials Vary

1. If different believers go through different kinds of trials, what does this mean?
   It means that we are diseased in different ways, requiring different treatments.

[6]
Like a Father

1. Does God want to destroy us?
   No, He is simply delivering us from the condemnation of the world.
2. If we don't receive this kind of chastisement, what does it mean?
   It means we are not true sons.

[7]
Suffering Persecution

1. What is the special badge of God's soldiery?
   Persecution.
2. What phrase makes you wonder about the American founders' familiarity with Calvin?
   "Our life, our fortunes, or our honor" is reminiscent of "our lives, our fortunes, our sacred honor" in the Declaration.

[8]
Consolation in God

1. Does the believer shrug suffering off as though it were nothing?
   No, Calvin says. What fortitude or moderation would there be in bearing such things with indifference?

2. What does the believer do with his bitter troubles?
   Valiantly resisting, he surmounts them.

[9]
Not Stoicism

1. What is the distinction between what Calvin urges here and Stoicism?
   The Christian gives expression to his pain and sorrow. He is not a stone.

2. What does Calvin identify as the Stoic's problem?
   He is a perfectionist, "too exact and precise."

3. What does Calvin call a contemporary form of neo-Stoicism?
   This iron philosophy.

[10]
Real Sorrow

1. Why was the apostle Peter pulled apart by a double will at his martyrdom, according to Calvin?
   Because he had not put off his human nature.

2. What do we do at the funerals of our dear ones?
   We weep the tears that are owed to our nature.

[11]
Fatalism Versus Faith

1. What reason for submitting does fatalism give?
   That it is useless to resist.

2. What reason does Calvin give?
   That God does nothing that does not proceed from a well-ordered justice, and that He intends our good and our benefit.

———— CHAPTER NINE ————

[1]

Present Vanity

1. Where does our blockishness arise?
   From the empty dazzlement of riches, power, and honors.

2. What is necessary before we are aroused to contemplate the life to come?
   Contempt for the present life.

[2]

Two Choices

1. There is no middle ground between what two options?
   Considering the world as worthless and having an intemperate love for it.

2. Do humans generally acknowledge the vanity of this life?
   Yes, but they never remember it.

[3]

Balance

1. Does contempt for this world mean ingratitude?
   No. Calvin is careful to teach that our recognition of the vanity of this world must not lead to hatred of the world or ingratitude against God.

[4]

Not Home Yet

1. If heaven is our homeland, then what must the earth be?
   It must be a place of exile.

[5]

Longing for Death

1. What does Calvin say of the man who does not joyfully await the day of death and final resurrection?
   He says he has made no progress in the school of Christ.

[6]

True Comfort

1. When we lift up our heads in hope, what are we enabled to see in right perspective?
   The wicked who take pride in the splendor and luxury of all their possessions.

CHAPTER TEN

[1]

Double Danger

1. What is the double danger Calvin warns against on material possessions?
   We have to guard against excessive strictness and excessive laxity both.
2. Can this be governed by a fixed rule?
   No, there is no definite or precise legal formula to bind the conscience.

[2]

The Main Point

1. What must we remember in the use of all things?
   The point God intended in giving them.
2. Did that include delight and pleasure?
   Yes. God clearly did not limit His gifts to mere function.

[3]

Insensibility

1. What does restriction to function do to a man?
   It reduces him to a block.
2. And what does the sweet smell of the kitchen do to another kind of man?
   It makes him unable to smell anything spiritual.

[4]

Pauline Balance

1. What Pauline principle does Calvin cite?
   From 1 Corinthians 7:29–31, he tells us that we should use things while sitting loose to them—those who buy, as if they had not bought, and so forth.

[5]
Going Without

1. How can we know if we can safely go with something?
   If we could safely go without it.

2. What is the third rule that Calvin mentions?
   Remembering that we must render an account of what we do; we are stewards.

[6]
Vocation

1. What else guides us in our use of things?
   Each man should look to his calling.

2. Is understanding our calling important?
   Yes—it is the beginning and foundation of well-doing.

———— CHAPTER ELEVEN ————

[1]
Justification and Regeneration

1. Because Christ was given to us, what double grace have we received?
   We are reconciled to God through Christ's blamelessness, and we are sanctified by Christ's Spirit. In short, we are justified and sanctified.

2. What is regeneration?
   The gift of being able to cultivate blamelessness and purity of life.

3. How important is justification to Calvin?
   It is the hinge on which religion turns.

[2]
The Threshold

1. Why do we need to get the concept of justification straight?
   So that we don't stumble at the very threshold.

2. How do we appear in God's sight as righteous, since we are sinners?
   We grasp the righteousness of Christ through faith and appear before God clothed in it.

3. What is justification?
The acceptance with which God receives us into His favor as righteous men.

[3]
Acquittal

1. Do we need to be innocent to be acquitted?
No, because Christ is righteous. Justification is nothing other than to acquit one who was accused, as if his innocence were confirmed. It is a judicial declaration.

[4]
The Precise Word

1. According to Calvin, does Scripture describe the reality of justification without using the word?
Yes. God has counted us acceptable *and* beloved *(Eph. 1:5–6). And in 2 Corinthians 5, the word* reconciled *means* justified.

[5]
Osiander's Errors

1. What does Calvin call Osiander's doctrine of essential righteousness?
He calls it "some strange monster."

2. What was Osiander's error?
He wanted justification to consist of the impartation of God's essential righteousness to us, and not Christ's obedience on the cross.

[6]
Confusion

1. What two things does Osiander confound?
Forgiveness of sins with rebirth.

2. What illustration does Calvin use of things that must be distinguished but which cannot be confused?
The light and heat from the sun. We can say they are inseparable, but we cannot say that heat lights the earth or that light heats it.

[7]
Faith

1. What does Calvin compare faith to?
   A vessel that holds something of much greater value.
2. What is faith, and what is its relation to Christ?
   Faith is the instrumental cause of our justification; Christ is the material cause.

[8]
Essential Righteousness

1. What is Osiander's view?
   That Christ, both God and man, is made righteousness for us with respect to His divine nature, and not His human nature.

[9]
Atonement

1. What is the basis for our justification that does not comport with the divine nature alone?
   Christ's atoning sacrifice. He died as a man.

[10]
Refuting a Slander

1. What slander does Calvin refute?
   Osiander's accusation that Calvin and those with him reckon faith as righteousness.
2. What does Calvin say is his highest glory?
   To be insulted by a proud man.

[11]
Assurance

1. Does Osiander accept or reject "justification" as a legal term?
   He rejects it, maintaining that in order to be declared righteous, one must be righteous.
2. What happens if faith pays any attention to works?
   Faith totters.

3. What is the wonderful plan of salvation?
That covered by the righteousness of Christ, we do not tremble at the judgment we deserve.

[12]
Refutation of Osiander

1. What is impossible, according to Osiander?
For God to regard as just any who are not just.

2. To what end does Osiander heap up passages that talk about righteousness?
To try to persuade his readers that whenever righteousness is mentioned, it means "essential righteousness."

[13]
Faith and Works Apart

1. What error does Calvin address next?
The notion that righteousness is composed of faith and works.

2. A man who wishes to obtain Christ's righteousness must do what?
Abandon his own righteousness.

3. As long as a particle of works righteousness remains, what else remains?
Some occasion for boasting.

[14]
Regenerate Works

1. What workaround to this did the Sophists come up with?
They suggest that we are justified by faith and works, provided they are the works given by grace after regeneration.

2. How does Calvin reply?
That Scripture says that the righteousness of faith is to believe that Christ died and rose again.

[15]
Impartation or Imputation

1. How do the Schoolmen interpret the grace of God?
As the Spirit helping in the pursuit of holiness, and not as the imputation of free righteousness.

2. What does Lombard do to Augustine?

Where Augustine is clear, Lombard muddles it. Where Augustine is slightly contaminated, Lombard corrupts it.

[16]

Sole Righteousness

1. What does the regenerate man trust in?

In the sole righteousness of Christ, and not in the good works toward which he inclines.

[17]

Faith Righteousness and Works Righteousness

1. How is faith said to justify?

Because it receives and embraces the righteousness offered in the gospel.

2. Why can the righteousness formed in us by the Spirit of God not be a cause of righteousness?

Because it is still imperfect.

[18]

Free Gift

1. What is Paul's argument on faith and works in a nutshell?

That if works are required for law righteousness, they must not be required for faith righteousness.

2. How must we come in order to receive righteousness?

We must come empty.

[19]

Faith Alone

1. Does Calvin agree with Luther's translation of Romans 3:28?

Yes, contextually.

2. What evasion does Calvin then deal with?

The idea that Paul is only excluding reliance on ceremonial works, not moral works.

[20]

Faith Working through Love

1. Does Calvin agree that justifying faith has to be the kind of faith that works through love (Gal. 5:6)?

Yes, but faith does not take its justifying power from that working.

[21]

Forgiveness

1. What is the righteousness of faith equated with?

Calvin equates it with forgiveness of sins.

2. What is such righteousness called?

Remission of sins.

[22]

Scripture Proofs

1. What passages does Calvin cite in defense of this idea?

He cites 2 Corinthians 5:21 and Romans 4:6–8.

2. Augustine says what about the righteousness of the saints?

He says it consists more of forgiveness than in perfection of virtues.

[23]

Righteousness of Another

1. How does this righteousness come to us?

By imputation, Calvin notes carefully.

2. What illustration does Ambrose use for this (an illustration that Calvin approves)?

That Jacob came in the clothing of another, smelling like another, in order to receive the blessing.

———— CHAPTER TWELVE ————

[1]

God's Tribunal

1. What happens when we evaluate ourselves before an earthly tribunal?

We think too highly of ourselves.

2. What do we miss until we come into the presence of God?
We miss that we are monstrously plagued with manifest diseases, and creak with defects beneath the skin.

[2]

Righteousness before Men

1. How may we come out ahead in moral comparisons of ourselves?
By making sure the comparison stops with men.

[3]

Devout Writers

1. Who are the two "devout writers" that Calvin cites?
Augustine and Bernard.

2. According to Bernard, what is "my merit"?
The Lord's compassion.

3. What does Calvin excuse as the "custom of the time"?
The use of "merits" for "good works."

[4]

Awakened Consciences

1. What do awakened consciences do?
Take safe refuge in God's truth, which is the only safe haven.

2. What is the actual state of what is considered righteousness before God?
It is sheer iniquity.

[5]

Away with Preening

1. We must consider ourselves without what two things?
Without flattery and without blind self-love.

2. What is there a need to strip bare?
The secret places of our depravity.

[6]

What Humility Is Not

1. What does Calvin refuse to identify as humility?
Any demeanor that leaves anything to ourselves.

2. What must you do if you want to be exalted with the humble?
Your heart must be wounded with the same contrition as theirs.

[7]
True Humility

1. Why was the publican who prayed in the Temple a sincere man?
Because he spoke testimonies of inner feeling.

[8]
Blockage

1. What blocks the way to Christ?
Arrogance and/or complacency.

2. What illustration does Calvin take from Bernard on the impossibility of taking credit for grace?
It is like a wall saying it gave birth to a sunbeam that passed through one of its windows.

———— CHAPTER THIRTEEN ————

[1]
Glory Undiminished

1. What two things does Calvin aim at in this section?
To see that God's glory remains undiminished, and that we can have consciences at rest.

2. Who rises up against God?
He who thinks he has anything at all of his own.

[2]
The Praise of Righteousness

1. Where must the praise of righteousness remain?
It must remain perfect and whole in the Lord's possession.

[3]
Unsettled Peace

1. How may a guilty conscience be quieted before God?
   By receiving unmerited righteousness.

[4]
Voiding the Promise

1. If we may depend upon works righteousness at all, what else happens?
   We make the promise void and without force.

2. Why does Calvin cite Augustine at this point?
   Lest anyone think he is saying something new.

[5]
Free Grace

1. What alone gives us peace of conscience and gladness in prayer?
   God's free grace alone.

———— CHAPTER FOURTEEN ————

[1]
Four Classes

1. What are the four classes of men outlined by Calvin?
   Those outside the Church entirely, those inside the Church who don't live it (both low-livers and hypocrites), and true Christians.

[2]
Virtues of Pagans

1. How does Calvin account for pagan virtues, where they exist?
   He says they are the gift of God.

2. Does he lump pagan vice and virtue all together?
   No, he says that would remove all order from the world.

3. What kind of blessing does God give such men?
   External blessing for a mere external conformity to His law.

[3]

True Virtue

1. Does Calvin account these pagan virtues as true virtue?
   No, because they proceed from perverse motives.

2. What is necessary for something to be truly virtuous?
   It has to be directed to the right end, that of serving God.

[4]

Limp on the Road

1. What illustration does Calvin take from Augustine here?
   That men of virtuous ability who do not serve Christ are men who can run fast, but they are not on the right road. And it is better to limp on the road than to run fast off of it.

[5]

Natural Condition

1. What must we set the grace of God against?
   The natural condition of man.

2. Where does our first capacity for well-doing come from?
   From regeneration.

[6]

Prior Condition

1. What were we before we were sprinkled through the Spirit with the blood of Christ?
   We were nothing other than sinners without Christ.

[7]

Impurity of Conscience

1. What do the two middle categories of Calvin's fourfold division have in common?
   Neither have been regenerated by the Spirit of God.

[8]

Hatred of Externals Only

1. What does the Lord abominate?
   The observance of His law when linked to personal iniquity.

2. What is man in his highest moral splendor?
   Still so far away from righteousness before the Lord that his virtues are reckoned sins.

3. What is the first foundation?
   True and living faith.

[9]

True Believers

1. What happens in believers each day?
   Their lusts are more and more mortified.

2. What are our best works mixed with?
   Some dregs are always mixed with them.

[10]

Just One Sin

1. What will just one sin do?
   Wipe out and extinguish every memory of previous righteousness.

[11]

The Pivotal Point

1. What is the believer's righteousness always to be considered?
   As faith righteousness, not works righteousness.

2. What two reasons keep a believer's work from being considered pure righteousness?
   First, it is corrupted in itself, and second, even if perfect, it would be corrupted by the surrounding sins.

3. What is the pivotal point of dispute with the Schoolmen?
   Whether renewal is to be considered as a part of justification.

[12]

Supererogation

1. What are works of supererogation?
   Works that rack up a surplus of merit.
2. Does Calvin allow for them?
   No, not at all.

[13]

Blunting the Edge of the Law

1. What tendency does holding to works of supererogation have?
   It tends to diminish the sharpness of God's demands and minimize the gravity of sin.
2. What position does Calvin reject with regard to those who keep the law partly?
   He rejects the idea that partial law-keeping results in righteousness by works to that extent.
3. What cannot overcome a single sin?
   Men's whole righteousness, gathered together in one heap.

[14]

Ne Plus Ultra

1. Is it possible to go beyond what God requires?
   No, after we have done everything, we still call ourselves "unworthy servants."
2. What should we not boast of?
   Voluntary liberality when we are actually constrained by necessity.

[15]

No Supererogation

1. What is the only kind of supererogation that Calvin allows?
   The kind spoken of by the prophet—"Who has required this at your hands?"

[16]

Two Plagues

1. What are the two plagues that we must banish from our minds?
   There must be no trust in works, and there must be no glory in works.

[17]

Four Causes

1. What are the four causes of our salvation?
   The efficient cause is the Father's love. The material cause is the Son's obedience. The instrumental cause is the Spirit's illumination in our hearts. The final cause is the glory of God's generosity.

2. What is not included in this list?
   Human works of any kind.

[18]

What Good Works Are Good For

1. In what two ways can believers refer to their own works?
   When contrasting them with the works of evil men, and when encouraging themselves in this evidence of God's election.

[19]

The Indwelling Spirit

1. What are the fruits of regeneration proof of?
   They are proof of the indwelling of the Holy Spirit.

[20]

Augustine's Prayer

1. What was Augustine's prayer with regard to works?
   That God see His works in Augustine's works—because if He saw Augustine's He would condemn it, and if He saw His own, He would crown it.

[21]

Good Works Rightly Understood

1. Does Scripture ever speak of good works in a causal way?
   Yes, Calvin acknowledges. But this is simply to speak of the "ordinary dispensation" of events, and not of ultimate causes which are entirely from God.

——————— CHAPTER FIFTEEN ———————

[1]

The Main Thing

1. For Calvin, what is justification by faith alone?
   It is the chief turning point.

[2]

A Pernicious Word

1. What problem does Calvin have with the use of the word "merit"?
   When applied to men's works over against God's judgment, it tends to mislead people.
2. Can someone use it without corrupting the gospel?
   Certainly. Calvin gives some examples of Augustine and Chrysostom.

[3]

Merit or Good Works?

1. If we don't use the word "merit," what place is there for good works?
   We have good works that God gives to us, and anything praiseworthy about them is due to God's grace.
2. What don't we do like the Sophists?
   We don't divide the credit for good works between God and man.

[4]

Two Appeals

1. How does Calvin handle the appeal from Ecclesiasticus?
   He forgoes his right to reject the authority of that book and mildly points out that if translated correctly, it loses its value to them as a proof text.
2. What is the problem with our good works?
   They are always spattered with much uncleanness.

[5]

The Sole Foundation

1. What is the sole foundation for our lives, according to Calvin?
   Jesus Christ.

2. What did Jesus not come to do?
   He did not come to help us attain righteousness but to be our righteousness.

3. If Christ is all, what follows?
   That we in ourselves have nothing.

[6]

Death and Life

1. What are those in the state of death unable to do?
   They are unable to beget the substance of life.

[7]

Mother of Errors

1. What is the mother of all errors?
   The schools of the Sorbonne.

2. What is the sum of all piety?
   Justification by faith alone.

3. What must happen in order for any good to proceed from us at all?
   We must be regenerated.

4. Does justification by faith alone prevent us from cheering the hearts of believers?
   No, not at all. But we do so without reference to our own merit, which would only unsettle everything.

[8]

Not a Finger-Breadth

1. What must we refuse to let happen?
   We must not allow ourselves to be drawn so much as a finger-breadth from this sole foundation.

——— CHAPTER SIXTEEN ———

[1]

Answering Slander

1. What slanderous charge does Calvin answer next?
   That justification by faith alone abolishes any need for good works.

2. How does Calvin answer this?

By pointing out that our justification is Christ, and we cannot receive Him without receiving all of Him. And He brings holiness of life with Him as well.

3. So what is the relationship of our salvation to our works?

It is not without works, yet not through works.

[2]
Zeal for Works

1. Does Calvin acknowledge rewards?

Yes, and chides his opponents for not being able to separate rewards from merit.

2. What is our calling?

Ours is a holy calling, one that demands purity of life and nothing less.

[3]
Judgment according to Works

1. Does Calvin acknowledge that God will render to each man according to his works?

Yes. But he denies that it is the principal thing.

2. What is necessary before men are fit to pursue holiness?

They must imbibe the doctrine of righteousness through Christ alone.

[4]
Free Grace

1. Is free grace free all around?

No. What is free for us cost Christ a great deal.

2. Our salvation is therefore too precious for what?

It is too precious to be matched by any compensation of works. We take refuge in God's mercy alone.

CHAPTER SEVENTEEN

[1]

Good Attitude toward Good Works

1. Justification is to be separated from good works for what three reasons?
   That we might not rely on them, glory in them, or ascribe salvation to them.

2. What is another argument for justification by works that Calvin answers here?
   That promises for faithful good works are attached to the commands of the law, and that justification by sheer grace would nullify those promises.

[2]

Works Do Not Attain the Promises

1. Why will we not attain to these promises through works?
   Because the promises have conditions, and we never meet those conditions.

2. What do we need in order to receive the promises?
   Another kind of righteousness, obtained through faith.

[3]

Fruitless Promises

1. Have these promises been given for no reason then?
   No, not at all. They are just fulfilled by a means other than works.

2. How are these promises fulfilled? What three conditions does Calvin set forth?
   First, that God justifies His servants apart from works. Second, God raises our works to a place of honor, doing so by grace, apart from the inherent value of these works. And third, He receives these works while pardoning their imperfections.

[4]

Cornelius

1. How does Calvin explain the fact that Cornelius was accepted by God (Acts 10:31)?
   By pointing out that Cornelius was already a converted man.

[5]
The Lord's Pleasure

1. Why is the Lord pleased with the good works of the believer?
   Because He cannot fail to love the good things He is doing in us.
2. What is regeneration?
   A renewal of the divine image in us.
3. How does God embrace our good works?
   In Christ.

[6]
Promises

1. Does Calvin acknowledge more than one kind of promise in the Old Testament?
   Yes. Some are promises of the law ("Do this and you will live"), while others are promises of grace.

[7]
Righteousness

1. Is conformity to the law sometimes called "righteousness"?
   Yes, as when someone returns a pledge to a poor man (Deut. 24:13).
2. Does Calvin reject what he calls law righteousness?
   No. He says he would accept it if it existed. But it doesn't; it is "nowhere visible."

[8]
Works Appraised

1. How are good works appraised by God?
   After forgiveness of sins, our good works are evaluated on a basis other than their own merits.

[9]
Foundation of Works

1. What relationship does justification by faith have to genuine good works?
   Justification by faith is the "beginning, foundation, cause, proof, and substance" of godly good works.

[10]

Prerequisites

1. What is necessary before works can be acceptable?
   Sins have to be pardoned.

2. Does justification cover our persons only?
   No, our works are justified as well as our persons.

[11]

James and Paul

1. What is the apparent conflict between James and Paul?
   Paul says we are justified by faith alone, and James seems to say we are not.

2. What is Calvin's starting assumption?
   That the two biblical writers do not conflict.

3. Those who set James against the doctrine of the Protestants are guilty of what?
   A "double fallacy." They misunderstand the word "faith" and the word "justify."

4. What kind of "faith" is James talking about?
   A boasting faith, a dead faith, a devil's knowledge. No surprise that it does not justify.

[12]

Different Kinds of Justification

1. Are Paul and James using the word "justify" in the same way?
   No, because Abraham was justified by faith before the birth of Ishmael, long before the sacrifice of Isaac. This means that James is speaking of the declaration of righteousness, not the imputation of it.

[13]

Romans 2:13

1. How does Calvin handle Romans 2:13?
   As a hypothetical situation, designed to convict those Jews who thought they were keeping the law simply by hearing it.

[14]

The Appeal to Works by Believers

1. How does Calvin handle the multiple places where believers appeal to God on the basis of their innocence?

He points to two particulars. The first is that sinful men may certainly protest their innocence with regard to a particular accusation (a theft, a murder, etc). This is a contextual plea. Secondly, they may protest their innocence in comparison to their accusers. This is a comparative plea. But in neither case is the believer claiming an absolute innocence.

[15]

Perfection

1. Does Calvin allow believers to claim any kind of perfection?

Only if they follow Augustine's definition, where he insists that any claim of perfection must recognize in truth and in humility the reality of the continuing imperfections.

——— CHAPTER EIGHTEEN ———

[1]

Recompense

1. How does Calvin explain those passages which say that God will repay every man according to his works?

By saying it refers to an order of sequence rather than causation.

2. How do we know that our good works are not meritorious in themselves?

Because the grace of God is conjoined to them (Jn. 6:27).

[2]

Inheritance

1. How is the term "reward" to be understood?

As the inheritance of a son, not the wages of a servant.

2. How do we know that Abraham did not earn the promise by his obedience with Isaac?

Because the promise was given to him years before.

[3]
Trained Well

1. What trains us to meditate on the fruition of our lives?
   Our good works have that training function.
2. Calvin quotes an early church writer to what effect?
   He quotes Pseudo-Ambrose who interpreted the parable of the workers in the vineyard as showing that those who had worked all day were as much recipients of grace as those who worked only the last part of the day.

[4]
The End of Scripture

1. What is the whole end of Scripture?
   To restrain our pride, to humble us, to cast us down, and to utterly crush us.
2. What must we not deduce from the concept of reward?
   We must not deduce merit. To do so wanders very far from God's plan.

[5]
Justified Works

1. How can God impute righteousness to our works?
   Only by having His compassion cover over the unrighteousness that remains within them.
2. How does a faith that is not reprobate work?
   It works through love.
3. The righteousness of good works depends upon what?
   It depends upon God pardoning them.

[6]
Generosity

1. How does one lend to the Lord?
   By giving to the poor.
2. Is this kind of generosity meritorious?
   No.
3. Why does God allow us to lay up treasures in heaven this way?
   Even though such gifts are unworthy even of His glance, He permits none of them to be lost.

[7]

Tribulation

1. What about tribulation? Doesn't God promise that He will not forget our sufferings?
   Yes, He does. But this promise, like all God's promises, would mean nothing unless God's mercies had gone before.

2. According to Augustine, in what sense is the Lord our debtor?
   The Lord made Himself our debtor, not by accepting anything from us, but by promising us all things.

[8]

Love

1. Is love greater than faith?
   Yes.

2. Does this mean that love can justify?
   No.

3. What illustration does Calvin use?
   The fact that a king is much greater than a cobbler does not mean he can make shoes better than a cobbler can.

4. If we were justified by our love, who would be justified?
   No one.

[9]

Keeping the Commandments

1. How does Calvin understand Matthew 19:17?
   Christ points the lawyer back to the law because he was not yet aware of his sinfulness.

[10]

Unbelief

1. In relationship to other sins, what is unbelief?
   It is the first defection from God.

2. For someone to be called righteous, what must their life be like?
   It must be a life that follows the divine will with unwavering and unwearying observance.

——— CHAPTER NINETEEN ———

[1]

Christian Liberty

1. How many aspects to Christian freedom are there?
   Calvin describes three.

2. Is Christian liberty important?
   Calvin says it is a "prime necessity."

3. What are the two errors he describes with regard to Christian liberty?
   Those who abuse it and those who reject it.

[2]

Justification

1. What is the first error he addresses?
   Tying our justification to performance of the law in any way.

[3]

Galatians

1. Is the letter to the Galatians simply about freedom from ceremonies?
   No. That is included, but the topic discussed is much loftier than that.

2. What is that loftier something?
   Freedom from the condemnation of the law in all things and in every respect.

[4]

Obedience apart from Law

1. What is true obedience?
   To love the Lord with all our hearts, apart from any concern about self-justification or law righteousness.

2. Does anyone do this fully?
   No. Those who have progressed farther than all others are still far away from this goal.

[5]

Sons and Servants

1. What two kinds of obedience does Calvin compare here?
   The obedience of servants and the obedience of sons.

2. What passage does Calvin cite to justify his statement of how God receives our labors?
   Malachi 3:17.

[6]

No Fear

1. What do we need not fear now that we have been emancipated by grace?
   The remnants of sin.

[7]

Things Indifferent

1. Why do we need to really understand the importance of what is "indifferent" and what is not?
   Because if we don't, there will be no end of superstitions.
2. What does Calvin understand about the nature of "scruples"?
   He knows they never end—a man "will not dare touch water if sweeter and cleaner than other water."

[8]

Freedom of Use

1. How should we use God's gifts?
   We should use them for the purpose for which He gave them.

[9]

Gluttony and Luxury

1. Are luxuries a thing indifferent?
   Yes, but only if they are used indifferently.
2. Has God forbidden us to use lovely things?
   Not at all. But we are not to wallow in them. We are not to luxuriate in them.

[10]

Remember the Weak

1. What other key element must we remember in using our liberty?
   We must never use it in a way that stumbles the weak.

[11]

Offenses

1. What fundamental distinction does Calvin make between different kinds of offenses?
   Between offenses given and offenses taken.
2. Who takes offense with each kind?
   Weak brothers and Pharisees respectively.

[12]

Right Use of Freedom

1. What two situations did Paul handle differently, but with "no change of purpose or mind"?
   The circumcision of Timothy and the refusal to circumcise Titus.

[13]

Limits

1. What limit is placed on our use of freedom?
   We must never use our freedom to offend against God.

[14]

The Free Conscience

1. From what is the believing human conscience freed by Christ?
   From the power of all men.

[15]

Two Kingdoms

1. What are the two kingdoms among men?
   Spiritual and temporal.
2. In which forum do we find each respectively?
   The inner and outer forum.

[16]

Conscience

1. What is a good conscience?
   Inward integrity of heart.

CHAPTER TWENTY

[1]

Faith and Prayer

1. How can the treasures of the Christian philosophy not be obtained?
   They cannot be wrested from a syllogism.

2. Once we have learned what we are in Christ, what are we to do?
   In prayer we are to ask of Him that we might be in Him what we are in Him.

[2]

Reaching Riches

1. What are we to do when God promises us something?
   We are to ask for it in prayer.

2. What is the result of prayer offered by burdened sinners?
   Extraordinary peace and repose.

[3]

Six Reasons

1. Calvin gives six motives to prayer. What are they?
   First, to fire our hearts with love. Second, to keep sin out. Third, that we might receive our benefits with gratitude. Fourth, that we might meditate upon His kindness. Fifth, that we may enjoy what we have received with delight. And last, that we might confirm His providence.

[4]

The First Rule of Prayer

1. What is the first rule for framing prayer?
   That we approach God with suitable reverence.

2. What model should we follow in prayer?
   The prayers of God's saintly servants in the Psalms.

3. What is the mind, when left to itself?
   A wanderer.

[5]

Disciplining Our Prayers

1. What is most contrary to reverence for God?
   Levity devoid of awe.

2. Why do we lift our hands in prayer?
   To remind us that we are far removed from God unless we raise our thoughts on high.

3. What are we not to ask?
   We are not to ask more than God allows.

[6]

The Second Rule

1. What is the second rule for framing prayer?
   That we always sense our own insufficiency.

2. How does Calvin describe cold-hearted prayer?
   That which does not ponder what it asks.

3. What do men do, stuffed with depravity?
   They ask for what they believe they already have, apart from God.

4. What is another fault, less serious, but no less tolerable?
   Mumbling prayers without meditation.

[7]

Foundation of Prayer

1. Do we pray according to the occasion?
   Yes, Calvin says, within limits.

2. Does this mean there are times when we need not pray?
   No. Calvin points out "there is no point of time when our need does not urge us to pray."

3. What does lawful prayer demand?
   Repentance.

[8]

The Third Rule

1. What is the third rule for prayer?
   Rejecting all self-confidence and seeking pardon and mercy.

2. Which Apocryphal book does Calvin quote with some approval?
   Baruch.

[9]

The Center of Prayer

1. What is the most important part of prayer?
   The plea for forgiveness.

2. Can we seek forgiveness without seeking deliverance?
   No. It would be absurd to want the effect to be removed without also removing the cause.

[10]

Confidence

1. What is meant when various saints in Scripture plead their own righteousness?
   As Calvin covered earlier, they are referring to their regeneration (itself a gift). Their purity is seen in contrast with the impurity of their enemies.

[11]

Fourth Rule

1. What is the fourth rule for prayer?
   That we should pray with a sure hope of answer.

2. What does lack of trust in prayer do?
   It provokes God.

3. What is our guide in prayer?
   Faith is our guide.

[12]

An Illustration

1. What comparison does Calvin use for us unburdening ourselves in prayer?
   We are like children unburdening themselves to their parents.

[13]

A Basic Motive

1. What should be our basic motive in praying this way?
   That God commands us to and promises a response.

[14]

Confident Prayer

1. What demeanor should we have in prayer instead of terror?
   Reverential fear.

2. Is this consistent with confidence?
   Yes, fully consistent.

3. Upon what does this confidence rest?
   Our prayers rest, not upon our own merit, but upon God's promises.

[15]

Defective Prayers

1. Why does God answer prayers from unbelievers that are clearly defective?
   To prove to His elect how easily entreated He is.

2. What are the prayers of the saints a mixture of?
   Faith and error.

[16]

Constant Forgiveness

1. How can our prayers obtain an answer?
   Only through God's forgiveness.

2. Does Calvin give any examples of intemperate prayers that are answered?
   Yes. Some of David's prayers, and one of Jeremiah's.

3. Should the defects in these prayers be repudiated?
   Yes, according to Calvin. But God pardons and receives them.

4. Is it legitimate to raise hands in prayer?
   Certainly, but not if you leave your heart on the ground.

[17]

Two Offices

1. What two offices of Christ are assumed when we pray in Jesus' name?
   The offices of advocate and mediator.

[18]

High Priest

1. In what way is Christ like the high priest of the Old Testament?
   He bears us into the presence of God, carrying us on His shoulders and breastplate.

[19]

If Christ Were Removed

1. If Christ were removed, what would remain for us at the throne of God?
   Wrath, judgment, and terror.

2. As we intercede for one another, what should we be careful to do?
   We should direct all our intercessions to the sole intercession of Christ.

[20]

One Mediator

1. What error of the Sophists does Calvin address next?
   That Christ is the mediator of redemption, but believers are the mediators of intercession.

2. Who alone bears the petitions of God's people to God?
   Christ alone.

[21]

Departed Saints

1. How would departed saints need to petition God?
   They would need to pray in Jesus' name also.

2. What is the import of this observation?
   If departed saints have to pray through Christ, then why should we not pray through Christ directly?

3. Why do people feel a need to enlist the saints?
   They are burdened by anxiety and believe Christ to be insufficient.

[22]

Veneration of Saints

1. What church council forbade directing prayers to the saints from the altar?
   The Council of Carthage.

[23]

Angels and Saints

1. What confusion is used by those who urge veneration of the saints?
   A confusion of departed spirits with angels. If that were true, then departed saints would be appointed to minister to us (Heb. 1:14).

[24]

Departed Saints

1. What would prayers to the departed saints do to "their own repose"?
   The saints would have to be drawn back into earthly cares.

2. And what do such prayers presuppose about the saints' abilities?
   That they have eyes keen enough to see our needs. In short, such prayer presupposes the saints have the attributes of deity.

[25]

Invocation of the Patriarchs

1. What did invocation of the patriarchs mean?
   Not that Israel was calling upon the patriarchs, but rather that God was being called upon to remember Abraham, Isaac, and Jacob.

2. Whose name should we rather put forward rather than Christ's? Anyone's?
   No one's.

[26]

Imitation of the Saints

1. When the Bible tells us the saints were heard by God, what did this not mean?
   It did not mean that only they would be heard.

2. What did it mean?
   It meant we should follow their example of faith.

[27]

Mother of Right Prayer

1. What is the mother of right prayer?
   Faith grounded upon the word.

[28]

Private Prayer

1. What should accompany our reception of all the blessings God gives?
   Continual thanksgiving.
2. If we fail to offer Him praise for His blessings, what is our silence?
   Our silence is spiteful.
3. Why do some mumble as they pray?
   Because of peevishness, boredom, impatience, bitter grief, and fear.

[29]

Public Prayer

1. Does God appoint public hours for prayer?
   No. The times are indifferent to God but are agreed upon by us for our convenience.
2. What are two kinds of corruption in public prayer?
   Saying over and over again the same little prayers and swelling up with a great mass of words.

[30]

Public Temples

1. What do we need to have since there needs to be common prayers for believers?
   There ought to be public temples.
2. Public prayer is lawful, provided what?
   Provided ostentation and chasing after paltry human glory are banished.
3. Do the buildings make prayers more holy?
   No, because we are the true temple.

[31]

Singing

1. Does Calvin condemn speaking and singing in church?
   No, he commends them, provided it comes from the heart.

[32]

Dignified Singing

1. What does music lend to sacred actions?
   It lends dignity and grace to them and has great value in kindling our hearts to zeal.

[33]

An Understandable Tongue

1. What language should public prayers be in?
   They should be in the common tongue.

2. What is the tongue without the mind?
   Highly displeasing to God.

3. What gestures does Calvin approve for prayer?
   Kneeling and uncovering the head.

[34]

The Lord's Prayer

1. The Lord's Prayer is a table of what?
   It is a table of all that the Lord allows us to request of Him.

[35]

Six Petitions

1. How many petitions does Calvin divide the Lord's Prayer into?
   He divides it into six instead of seven.

2. How are those six divided?
   Like the Ten Commandments. The first three concern God directly, the last three concern ourselves.

[36]

In Calling Him Father

1. What are we doing when we call God Father?
   We are putting the name of Christ forward.

2. How does Calvin describe the name of Father?
   As a name of great sweetness.

[37]

Encouraged

1. What should encourage us about our use of the name Father?
   We should be encouraged that God the Father is compassionate, as was the father in Christ's parable.

[38]

Our Father

1. What is significant in the word "our"?
   This means that we have brothers, and that there should be brotherly love among us.

2. If you love the Father, what follows?
   You love His children.

[39]

Prayer and Almsgiving

1. How is prayer like almsgiving?
   Just as you can't give alms to every poor person in the world, so you can't pray for everybody.

2. What shuts the gate to prayers?
   Strife.

[40]

In Heaven

1. Though God is in heaven, what does Calvin want us to recognize?
   That He is not bound there.

[41]

The First Petition

1. What is the first petition of the Lord's Prayer?
   That God's name be hallowed.

2. What are we always bidden to be concerned for in our prayers?
   God's holiness.

[42]

The Second Petition

1. What is the second petition?
   That God's kingdom come.

2. What relation does the second petition have to the first?
   They are almost identical.

3. How does God set up His kingdom?
   By humbling the whole world in different ways.

[43]

The Third Petition

1. What is the third petition?
   That God's will be done on earth as it is in heaven.

2. What does this tell us about God's kingdom?
   It tells us that God will be king of the world when all submit to His will.

3. What can be said about those who do not pray for these things?
   That they are not to be reckoned among God's children and servants.

[44]

The Fourth Petition

1. What do we do in the second half of the prayer?
   We descend to our own affairs.

2. What is the fourth petition?
   Our request for our daily bread.

3. What do some who entrust their souls to God still struggle with?
   They are still troubled about the flesh.

4. When our storehouses are stuffed and our cellars full, what should we still do?
   We must still seek our daily bread.

[45]

The Fifth Petition

1. What is the fifth petition?
   That God forgive our debts.

2. Why does He call sins debts?
   Because we owe penalty for them.

3. What do people who offer their own merits to God do?
They call for His judgment, instead of entreating mercy.

[46]
The Sixth Petition

1. What sort of gain should we pursue?
Only that which is lawful and honest.

2. What do greedy men look like?
They madly scrape together from everywhere, by fair means or foul.

3. What should we do if we have to contend with faithless and deceitful men?
Give up something rather than contend with them.

[47]
Public Prayers

1. What should the prayers of Christians be?
They should be public.

2. What is signified by the "amen"?
The warmth of our desire.

[48]
The Sum of the Acceptable

1. What is the Lord's Prayer a summary of?
It is a summary of all that is acceptable in prayer.

[49]
Verbatim

1. Must we be entirely limited to the words of the Lord's Prayer?
No. We may pray for these things in our own words.

2. What should no man ask for?
"Anything at all except what is included by way of summary in this prayer."

[50]
Weakness in Prayer

1. What is necessary because of our weakness in prayer?
Many aids and supports.

2. What is one such aid and support?
   Prayer at regular times—before work, before meals, etc.
3. And at the same time, what should be avoided?
   Superstitious observance of hours.

[51]

Futility

1. What do our prayers sometimes appear to be?
   Our prayers sometimes appear to be beating the air.

[52]

Kindly Reception

1. When God refuses to comply with our wishes, what is His disposition toward us?
   He is still attentive and kindly to our prayers.

——— CHAPTER TWENTY-ONE ———

[1]

Predestination

1. What reveals the wonderful depth of God's judgment?
   The variations in the preaching of the gospel, and the varied responses among those to whom it is preached.
2. What are two characteristics of the doctrine?
   It is useful, and it is sweet fruit.
3. What tears humility up by the roots?
   Getting rid of the doctrine of predestination.
4. What are the three benefits?
   God's free mercy, God's glory, and sincere humility.
5. What happens if men pry too deeply into the subject?
   They get lost in a labyrinth.

[2]

The Rule for Discussion

1. Where do we learn about predestination?
   We should learn from Scripture alone.

2. What sort of result comes from this?
We achieve a learned ignorance.

[3]
Excessive Avoidance

1. What do some men do with the subject?
They avoid it, as mariners would a reef.

2. What is Scripture?
It is the school of the Holy Spirit.

3. So how far may we go in discussion of this topic?
As far as this curriculum takes us.

[4]
Alleged Peril

1. What will obstinate people do with the doctrine of predestination?
They will mock it.

2. Should this prevent us from teaching it?
No, because the same thing can be done with other basic doctrines.

3. What are several of these other doctrines?
The doctrine of the Trinity and that of young-earth creation.

4. Why can we safely follow Scripture in this?
Because Scripture proceeds as a mother stooping so that her child can keep up—as Augustine put it.

5. In what way do opponents of this doctrine accuse God of stupid thoughtlessness?
They talk as though God had not seen the peril that they have so wisely met.

[5]
Foreknowledge and Predestination

1. Considering foreknowledge and predestination, what is to subject one to the other?
Absurd.

2. How does Calvin define predestination?
As God's eternal decree, "by which He compacted with Himself what He willed to become of each man."

3. Arguments against God's sovereignty will not strike or hurt His righteousness—why?
Because arguing this way is like throwing rocks at heaven. They only fall back on you.

[6]

The Second Degree

1. What is the second, more limited degree of election?
God's special grace for those who will be eternally saved.

2. What then are the two degrees?
An election to national or corporate grace is the first, and personal election to salvation the second.

[7]

Election Proper

1. What is only half explained?
Election, until we come to individual persons.

2. How does Calvin explain what makes up this individual election?
He calls it "ascending to the Head," which creates an indissoluble bond.

3. What enables the elect to persevere to the very end?
The spirit of regeneration.

———— CHAPTER TWENTY-TWO ————

[1]

Election or Foreknowledge

1. What do some do because God chooses some and passes over others?
They bring an action against Him.

2. What do Calvin's opponents needs to explain and answer?
Why they are men rather than oxen or asses.

3. Who is the principal beneficiary of election?
The man, the Lord Jesus Himself, who was not made Son of God by righteousness living.

[2]

Prior Distinction

1. What distinction can be made among those who do not yet exist?
None.

[3]

Election to Holiness

1. Why are we not elect because of our holiness?
Because we were elected to holiness.

[4]

Special Election

1. In what way are all the children of Abraham holy?
By virtue of the covenant.

2. Why do some of the "holy seed" degenerate from legitimate children to bastards?
Because God's special election towers and rules over all.

3. If Jacob were chosen on the basis of foreseen worth, what did Paul say to no purpose?
That Jacob had not yet been born when the choice was made.

[5]

What Is Foreseen

1. What good can God foresee in us?
Only the good that He Himself has determined to bestow.

[6]

Jacob's Blessing

1. Why was Jacob's blessing not to be considered as merely to earthly prosperity?
Because his election obtained for him a great deal of earthly troubles.

2. What does it mean that God has mercy on whom He will have mercy?
It means that God finds in men themselves no reason to bless them.

3. From what vantage does God not watch the future?
From an idle watchtower.

[7]

Christ's Testimony

1. What is the beginning of our reception into the surety and protection of Christ?
   The Father's gift.

2. What is not the reason that some excel?
   Their own effort or diligence.

[8]

The Fathers on Foreknowledge

1. Which church fathers appealed to God's foreknowledge of grace used well?
   Ambrose, Origen, Jerome, and the early Augustine.

2. What is Calvin's "the dog that did not bark" argument against this view?
   That if this were the case, Paul should have presented that answer in Romans 9 after raising the objection, "Is there injustice with God?"

3. What is the relationship between God's grace and our fitness?
   As Augustine said, "God's grace does not find but makes us fit to be chosen."

[9]

Thomist Subtlety

1. What does Calvin do with Thomas' argument that merit is not the cause of predestination on God's side, but it may be spoken of that way on our side?
   He dismisses it as an evasion. And he answers it by saying that predestination to grace could be made subordinate to predestination to glory, which would make Thomas's argument fall apart.

[10]

Universality of the Promise

1. What is Calvin's basic answer to those who say the universality of the promise nullifies special election?
   Calvin cites Scripture that shows God's distribution of grace not being conducted on egalitarian grounds (e.g., Acts 16:7ff).

2. What is the mother of faith?
   Election.

[11]
Patronizing the Apostle

1. In what way do we wrong and patronize the apostle Paul?
   By pretending that what is obvious to us was invisible to him.

2. What central argument does Calvin repeat here?
   If those who want our merits considered are in the right, then why did Paul not give this answer in Romans 9?

——— CHAPTER TWENTY-THREE ———

[1]
The Other Side of the Coin

1. What does human understanding do when it hears the truths of election?
   It breaks forth into "random and immoderate tumult as if at the blast of a battle trumpet."

2. If God passes over someone instead of electing him, what does that amount to?
   It amounts to condemnation.

3. Is hardening in the hand of God?
   Absolutely.

4. Is the relationship of God to good and evil the same?
   No. Calvin points out that Paul softens the expression when talking about hardening, but not in a way that moves the ultimate outcome away from the will of God.

5. So what is the cause of the hardening?
   The secret plan of God.

[2]
God's Will the Rule

1. What do the pious and moderate remember?
   That they are but men.

2. What is the highest rule of righteousness?
   The will of God.

3. What cannot be found?
   Anything higher than God's will.

4. Is God therefore lawless and a law unto Himself?
   No. He is free of all fault. But He still owes an accounting to no one.

[3]
Arguing with God

1. What does Calvin invite the sons of Adam to do?
   To come forward and quarrel with God.

2. As they attempt it, what do they deliberately suppress?
   The cause of their condemnation, which is in themselves.

[4]
God's Decree and His Justice

1. What argument do these people then resort to?
   They say yes, but the condemnation which they fall under was also foreordained for them.

2. Does Calvin agree that we are fallen in accordance with the will of God?
   Yes.

3. How does Calvin answer this?
   The same way Paul does—by appealing to the prerogatives of God. And he denies that he is resorting to a loophole. What stronger reason can be brought forward "than when we are bidden to ponder who God is"?

4. What may we not do if we fail to understand something of God's will?
   We may not condemn Him just because we are ignorant.

[5]
Shared Humanity

1. Can we know that God has willed these things?
   Yes. He has revealed so much.

2. Can we know why?
   No. It is "not for our reason to inquire."

3. How does Augustine answer when challenged on this point?
   He said that he too is a man. Therefore we should both listen to the one who says, "O man, who are you?"

4. What should we do with these things?
   We should imitate the apostle Paul and rest in the wonder.

[6]
Man's Responsibility

1. What is the next objection to election that Calvin answers?
   The idea that election removes man's responsibility.

2. Does Calvin agree that foreknowledge by itself is not deterministic?
   By itself, yes. But he notes dryly that God foreknows "by reason of the fact that he decreed."

[7]
A Predestined Fall

1. Does Calvin grant that the decree is dreadful?
   Yes, he calls it decretum horribile.

2. If there were a legitimate complaint, where would it have to lodged?
   Against predestination.

[8]
Willing and Permitting

1. Does Calvin grant a distinction between the will of God and the permission of God?
   No. There is no distinction.

2. What must be just?
   That which deserves praise.

3. Where should we focus our attention when contemplating the cause of our condemnation?
   In the corrupt nature of humanity, which is closer to home.

4. What is it to stay out of God's decrees, and what is it to pry?
   Ignorance is learned, and the craving to know is a "kind of madness."

[9]
Another Objection

1. Does Calvin think he is able to silence the objectors?
   No, because impiety will always have something to growl and mutter about.

2. What is it to act perversely in this?
   To seek out the source of your own condemnation by looking at the "hidden sanctuary of God's plan."

[10]

Yet Another Objection

1. What is a third objection that Calvin must answer?
   It is that election makes God a respecter of persons, contrary to what Scripture says about Him.
2. How does Calvin answer this?
   By saying that if the cause for the distinction is not found in man, then the respecting must not be of man.

[11]

No Injustice

1. When God chooses some for life and others not, why is He free from accusation?
   He does not owe forgiveness. He is like a lender who has the authority of remitting payment for one and not for another.

[12]

Not Encouraging Carelessness

1. What is the next objection to this teaching?
   That if it is taught, then zeal for doing good disappears.
2. Does Calvin acknowledge that some distort the doctrine this way?
   Yes, he says, "Many swine . . . pollute the doctrine of predestination with their foul blasphemies."
3. But what does Paul say we have been chosen to?
   To a holy and blameless life.

[13]

Meaningful Admonition

1. What is another related objection?
   That it discourages teachers from moral admonition.
2. How does Calvin answer this?
   He points to Paul, who taught this doctrine, and asks if Paul was cold in his admonitions and exhortations.

[14]

Prudence

1. What example of balance does Calvin point to?
Augustine, who taught this doctrine clearly, but in ways that would not give unnecessary offense.

———— CHAPTER TWENTY-FOUR ————

[1]

Election and the Call

1. Why does God teach His elect?
In order to lead them to faith.

2. Can grace be received by a hard heart?
No. Grace is given first to take that hardness away.

3. What does Scripture couple together so that we know that free mercy is to be sought?
The call and election.

4. How does Augustine turn around the view that "willing and running" are useless unless mercy is present?
By pointing out that this means that mercy is useless unless willing and running are present. And that is manifestly impious.

[2]

Grace Alone

1. What is a pledge of salvation that cannot deceive us?
The inner call.

[3]

Faith and Election

1. Does grace merely give us the ability to believe or not?
No. Grace gives us faith itself.

2. Does election take effect only after we believe?
No, not at all.

3. Can we take assurance from the fact that we believe?
Certainly, for if we try to penetrate God's eternal ordination, we will be swallowed by an abyss.

4. What do some men do in order to make sure about God's plan?
They flit above the clouds, instead of heeding the word which is near us, in our hearts and mouths.

[4]
Attaining Certainty

1. What is a grievous error concerning election, one that Satan loves?
The error of trying break into the inner recesses of divine wisdom.

2. What question must we avoid?
What revelation do you have of your election?

3. What is the greatest and most pestilential error?
Investigating God's eternal plan apart from His word.

4. Where should we begin and end?
With the call of God, that comes through the word.

[5]
In Christ Alone

1. Where is election alone to be found?
In Christ alone.

2. Who alone is the fountain of life?
Christ.

3. If we have been chosen in Christ, where will we not find assurance?
We will not find assurance in ourselves.

4. If we want more than to be sons and heirs, what would we have to do?
We would have to rise above Christ, which is impossible.

5. What would be a preposterous prayer?
"Lord, if I am chosen, hear me."

6. Instead of praying this way, what should we be content with?
The promises of the word.

[6]
True Christians

1. Where does Christ bring those that He has truly illumined with the knowledge of His name?
Into the bosom of His Church.

2. If we want assurance, what should we embrace?
Christ.

3. What does Paul magnificently lord it over?
   Life and death, things present and to come.

4. What gift does this kind of boasting depend on?
   The gift of perseverance.

[7]

Apostasy

1. How then do we account for various apostasies that we have all seen?
   Those who fall away never cleaved to Christ "with the heartfelt trust" that the certainty of election provides.

2. What must we have instead of "crass and sheer confidence of the flesh"?
   We must have simple confidence, responding to the word.

[8]

Called and Chosen

1. How are we to understand Christ's statement that many are called but few are chosen?
   By realizing that there are two kinds of calls.

2. What is the first kind of call?
   The general call which God extends to all indiscriminately through the preached word. This even includes those for whom that word is the savor of death.

3. What is the second kind of call?
   The special call, which is accompanied by the inward illumination of the Spirit.

4. Is this special call for the true believer alone?
   Calvin says "for the most part."

5. Can anyone apostatize from this special call?
   A few. God illumines some temporarily but then "justly forsakes them for their ungratefulness."

6. Putting this together, who then cannot fall away?
   The one who has received this special call along with the gift of perseverance.

[9]

Judas

1. Was Judas one of Christ's sheep?
   No, but he occupied the place of one.

2. Did Jesus know this when He chose him to be an apostle?
   Yes (Jn. 6:70; 13:18).

3. When predestination is rightly understood, does it shake our faith?
   No. Rather it provides its best confirmation.

[10]

Before the Call

1. Before one of the elect is called, is there any difference between him and any of the nonelect?
   None at all.

2. How does Calvin show this?
   By citing multiple Scripture texts.

[11]

Not Growth from Seed

1. How does Calvin describe what happens to the elect?
   As deliverance from evil, instead of maturation into a good that they had in seed form.

[12]

Preaching to a Hundred

1. If the same sermon is preached to a hundred, and twenty believe, what needs to be explained?
   Not the eighty. They remain in unbelief according to their nature. What needs to be explained is the belief of the twenty, and the only explanation is the intervention of God.

[13]

Abandoned in Unbelief

1. According to Augustine, could God have turned the will of evil men to good?
   Of course.

2. Why, then, does He not?

Because, as Augustine put it, "He wills otherwise."

[14]

What the Impious Do

1. What do the impious do when they hear of God's sovereignty in salvation?

They "complain that God with unbridled power abuses His miserable creatures for His cruel amusement."

2. In contrast, what should we be willing to admit?

Ignorance where God's wisdom rises to its height.

[15]

Other Passages

1. What problem does Calvin address next?

The problem of passages that seem to contradict what he has been saying, like Ezekiel 33:11.

2. How does Calvin answer?

By showing that if God wills the wicked to live, without exception, this is not consistent with His behavior elsewhere (Mt. 11:23). If the inhabitants of Sodom would have responded more favorably to more grace than they got, then why did they not get more?

[16]

Another Passage

1. How does Calvin handle 1 Timothy 2:3–4?

The first way is the same as in the previous section—if God wants everyone saved equally, why doesn't He act like it?

2. What is the second way he responds?

He points out that such passages are talking about classes of people, kings and such.

[17]

One Last Objection

1. What two elements of the problem does Calvin grant?

He grants that God has a will that divides the human race into elect and reprobate, and he grants that God causes the gospel to be preached indiscriminately to all.

2. What is his final conclusion?
That we should tremble with Paul at so great a mystery.

——— CHAPTER TWENTY-FIVE ———

[1]

Resurrection Hope

1. Why is it hard for us to hope and trust in the coming resurrection?
Because we are slow and must climb over innumerable obstacles.

[2]

Receiving Christ's Benefits

1. Who alone receives the fruit of Christ's benefits?
Those who raise their minds to the resurrection.

[3]

Christ the Pioneer

1. Does Calvin acknowledge the difficulty of believing in the resurrection?
Yes, he does.

2. What are the two main helps that God gives to us?
The first is the parallel of Christ's resurrection; the second is the omnipotence of God.

3. What do scorners do with the Evangelists' history?
They treat it as a fairy tale.

[4]

God's Power

1. Why does Calvin argue that faith in the resurrection depends on faith in God's omnipotence?
Because that is what Paul says in Philippians 3:21.

[5]

Burial Rites

1. How does Calvin answer pagan unbelievers who deny the resurrection?
By pointing out that their universal custom of burial makes them profess what no one admits to believing.

[6]
Intermediate State

1. What does Calvin teach about the intermediate state?
   Not very much, because it is important not to go beyond what is written. But he says we know enough to say that we will be received by the Father of the faithful.

[7]
This Same Body

1. What does Calvin do with the idea that God gives us a completely new body, made from scratch?
   He rejects it as a monstrosity.

2. Why is the promised "change of quality" important in this?
   If we had completely new bodies, there would be no transformation. But transformation is what is promised.

3. What is Calvin's argument from headship on this?
   If we get new bodies, and not our old bodies raised and transformed, then head and body do not match. Christ's old body was raised and transformed.

[8]
Burial Rites

1. What is the mother of this notion?
   Unbelief. Unbelief cannot handle the idea that bodies, exposed so long to corruption, could be restored.

2. How does Calvin answer?
   With Scripture. For example, Romans 8:11 says that God will give life to our mortal bodies.

3. Does Calvin think burial rites are superstitious?
   No. He thinks they are a testament to the reality of the resurrection.

[9]
The Resurrection of the Wicked

1. Does Calvin hold to a resurrection of the ungodly?
   Yes, on the basis of numerous scriptural statements.

2. How can resurrection, a benefit of Christ's resurrection, be extended to the ungodly?

It extends to them, not to become their lawful possession, but rather "to render them inexcusable."

[10]

Eternal Blessedness

1. How did the prophets describe our eternal state?

Because of our limitations, they describe our blessedness under physical terms.

2. What must we not be titillated by?

An immoderate desire to know more than is lawful.

3. Does Calvin believe that everyone will have equal measures of glory in heaven?

No, and he cites Scripture to this effect. Two jars can be completely full of happiness, full to capacity, and be differently sized jars.

[11]

Superfluous Questions

1. Who inquires into the different glory rankings between apostle and prophet, apostle and martyr, and so on?

Men hungry for empty learning.

2. What faults in the creation are repaired in the resurrection?

Those which took their beginning from sin.

[12]

The Lot of the Damned

1. How are the torments of the lost described for us in Scripture?

Again, as with the saved, by means of physical images.

2. What are these images intended to do?

To confound all our senses with dread.

3. For Calvin, what is the heart of damnation?

Being excluded from the presence of the Lord and from the glory of His might (2 Thes. 1:9).

BOOK FOUR

THE EXTERNAL MEANS OR AIDS

*by which God invites us into
the society of Christ and holds us therein*

—————— CHAPTER ONE ——————

[1]

The Holy Catholic Church

1. How does Christ become ours?
   Through faith in the gospel.
2. But what do we need because of our ignorance and sloth?
   We need outward helps.
3. Why sacraments?
   To foster and strengthen faith.
4. What has the papacy done?
   It has polluted everything God had appointed for our salvation.
5. If God is your Father, who may you call your Mother?
   The holy catholic Church.

[2]

Church and Creed

1. What does the phrase "I believe the church" refer to?
   To the visible and invisible church both.
2. Which reading of that phrase does Calvin prefer?
   He prefers "I believe the church," not "I believe in the church."
3. Why is the Church called catholic or universal?
   Because there could not be two or three churches.

[3]

Communion of Saints

1. What principle governs God's gifts to us?
   Whatever He gives to us, we should bestow on one another.

2. Should we try to distinguish elect and reprobate?
   No, that is for God alone to do.

[4]

The Visible Church

1. What title describes the visible church?
   Mother.

2. Is there another way of salvation outside this mother?
   No.

3. How long must we be under her authority?
   All our lives.

[5]

Ministers of God

1. How has God determined to grow us up to maturity, compared to how He could have done it?
   He has done it through the education of the church, when He could have done it by divine fiat.

2. Why does God consecrate the mouths and tongues of men?
   In order that His voice may resound in them.

3. What do some stubborn men refuse to do?
   They refuse to submit to being taught by human word and ministry.

4. How is the church built up?
   Solely by outward preaching.

5. What must all in the church do, from the highest to the lowest?
   Aspire to the Head.

[6]

Boundaries and Limits

1. Who is the author of preaching?
   God.

2. Is the preacher anything apart from the work and blessing of God?
   Nothing.

[7]
Visible and Invisible

1. What church is actually "in God's presence"?
   The church in which no one is received unless they have been made true children of God by the Holy Spirit.

2. What church has many hypocrites mingled in with it?
   The visible church.

[8]
Limitations of Judgment

1. What does Augustine say about the perspective of God's secret predestination?
   He looks at the church and sees many sheep outside the church and many wolves within.

2. So on what basis do we receive others as fellow Christians?
   On the basis of charitable judgment.

[9]
Marks of the Church

1. Where does a church of God exist?
   Where the word is purely preached and the sacraments administered according to Christ's institution.

2. May we receive as brothers those that we believe to be living in a manner unworthy of it?
   Yes, because of the common agreement of the church. Until that status is lawfully removed, we should honor it.

[10]
The Sin of Schism

1. Since God has so clearly marked His Church, how serious is it to separate from a true church?
   It amounts to a denial of God and Christ.

[11]
The Marks Under Attack

1. What two devices does Satan use to assault the marks of the Church?
   He either corrupts them entirely, or he corrupts them to such an extent that people abandon the true church prematurely.

[12]

Guarding against Schism

1. Should we reject a church that still retains the marks?
   No, not even if it otherwise swarms with faults.

2. Are all doctrines of equal weight?
   No. Some are fundamental—God is one, Christ is God, salvation by God's mercy, and so forth. Some are not essential to the sum of religion.

[13]

Scandal

1. What sort of men leave a church because they found some sin in it?
   Calvin calls them airy spirits.

2. Do they have a legitimate complaint?
   They often do. But the legitimate complaint against some fault leads to an illegitimate conclusion that this fault negates the identity of the church.

3. What do they substitute for kindness?
   Immoderate severity.

[14]

The Problem of Corinth

1. If imperfections could remove a church's identity as a church, what would have happened to Corinth?
   They would have been no church at all because of their grievous problems.

2. But what does Paul call them?
   A church of Christ and communion of saints (1 Cor. 1:2).

3. What remained intact at Corinth?
   The ministry of the word and the sacraments.

[15]

Fellowship with the Wicked

1. Does Calvin allow that it is a disgrace for the faithful to be forced to share table fellowship with those who ought to be excommunicated?
   Yes, it is a great evil. But it would be a greater evil to separate from the church because of it.

2. Should faithful Christians avoid friendship with such persons?
   Yes. But they should not renounce the communion of the church.

3. Who should we examine when we come to the Lord's Table?
   Ourselves. We don't examine everybody else.

4. Who has the authority to determine who should be received and who rejected?
   That belongs to the church as a whole, in accordance with lawful order.

[16]

False Perfection

1. Where does perfectionism that results in splits come from?
   It arises from pride and arrogance.

2. Is it driven by true hatred of iniquity in others?
   No, but is rather driven by a hankering after their own contentions.

[17]

Real Holiness

1. If we will not admit a church unless it is perfect in every respect, what will happen?
   We will admit no church at all.

[18]

Prophetic Example

1. What did the prophets not do in response to the corruptions of Israel?
   They did not establish new churches or erect new altars.

[19]

Christ and the Apostles

1. How did Christ and the apostles respond to the desperate impiety of the Pharisees?
   By continuing to practice the same rites among the people.

2. Who owns the breaking of earthen vessels?
   According to Cyprian, this belongs to the Lord alone.

3. What does Calvin say about someone who leaves a church where the word is preached and sacraments are administered?
   He says they are without excuse.

[20]
A Devilish Invention

1. What is a devilish invention?
   Being cocksure about our own perfection while part of this earthly race.

2. What is the first entry into the church, and what should therefore be the principal mark of holiness?
   Forgiveness of sins.

[21]
Lasting Forgiveness

1. Is forgiveness the basis for more than our entry into the church?
   Yes. Our continuance in the church is also dependent upon forgiveness. The Lord sustains us by means of forgiveness.

[22]
Power of the Keys

1. What was the basic reason God gave the ministers of the church the power to absolve sins?
   Not so much for bringing unbelievers into the church, but rather that they should continually discharge this ministry among believers.

2. In what settings do ministers absolve sins?
   Both publicly and privately.

3. What are the three basic principles involved?
   First, believers cannot stand before God without ongoing forgiveness. Second, we cannot enjoy this blessing apart from communion with the church. Third, it is dispensed to us through the preaching of the word and the administration of the sacraments.

[23]
All Believers Seek Forgiveness

1. What do some rigorists pretend?
   They pretend that after baptism, no Christian can sin. If they do, they fall away irrevocably.

2. How often does the Lord require believers to confess their sins?
   Continually, throughout their lives.

[24]

Grace to the Patriarchs

1. What does Calvin call the time of the patriarchs?
   The swaddling clothes of the Church.

2. Whose sins are outlined as grievous?
   The sins of the patriarchs, the twelve sons of Israel.

3. What did God do for these men?
   He raised them up as heads.

[25]

Grace in the Prophets

1. What prophets does Calvin cite to show the ongoing grace of God in forgiveness?
   He cites Jeremiah 3:1 and Ezekiel 18:23.

2. How is grace shown in the dedication of the Temple?
   Solomon clearly declares the provision made for ongoing sin.

[26]

Grace in the New Covenant

1. What does Calvin find unthinkable?
   That grace would have been manifest in the Old Testament and then taken away after Christ came.

[27]

Grace to Churches

1. What examples of grace to delinquent churches does Calvin cite?
   He cites the examples of the Galatians and Corinthians.

[28]

Sins of Ignorance

1. What do some of the more prudent rigorists say?
   That God does forgive unconscious sins this way, but not sins committed knowingly and willingly.

2. How does Calvin reply?
   By showing that in the law, God forgave both kinds of sin.

[29]

The Ancient Church

1. How does Calvin handle the view of the early church fathers on "second repentance"?

By showing that they agreed with him on sins they called "slight errors," which were actually pretty serious sins, in order to distinguish them from public crimes which required church discipline.

─────────── CHAPTER TWO ───────────

[1]

The Basic Issue

1. What sorts of errors are to be pardoned in a church?
Those which do not harm the chief doctrine of religion.

2. What is it that causes the death of a church?
When falsehood breaks into the citadel of religion, the sum of necessary doctrine is overturned, and the right use of the sacraments is destroyed.

3. When must a church tumble down?
When the sum of religion is destroyed.

[2]

Claims of Rome

1. What does Calvin conclude then about Rome?
You can see for yourself how much of a church remains there.

2. What is the basic argument that Romanists put forward?
That of antiquity and a succession of bishops.

[3]

A False Church

1. Who argued in a similar way to the Romanists?
The Jews at the time of Jeremiah, who boasted of the Temple, ceremonies, and priestly functions.

2. Did the Jews lack anything with regard to an outward church?
Nothing.

3. What is Calvin's argument from Ishmael?
He was a member in that he was circumcised, and with regard to antiquity, he was firstborn.

4. What is the absurdity that Calvin addresses?
It is absurd to lodge succession in persons alone in exclusion to teaching.

[4]
Founded on the Word

1. What do the Romanists do to the uneducated?
Frighten them with the name of the church.

2. How do the words of Jesus support what Calvin says about the Church?
He identifies His sheep by who listens to His voice.

3. What is the scepter Christ uses to rule in His Church?
His holy word.

[5]
Heresy and Schism

1. What are the two bonds that hold a communion together?
Agreement in doctrine and brotherly love.

2. What is the difference Augustine makes between heretics and schismatics?
The former sin against doctrine, while the latter sin against love.

[6]
Unity in the Head

1. How does Cyprian account for the unity and diversity of the Church?
The unity is found in its common connection to the Head, Christ, and the diversity is found as the Church takes its forms according to circumstance.

2. What does Calvin point out about their separation from Rome?
He says it was like the case of the apostles, who were forced out. They did not leave but were expelled. But Calvin adds that to find Christ, he would have been willing to leave.

[7]

An Old Testament Roman Church

1. Rome resembles Israel under which ruler?
Jeroboam.

[8]

Gradations of Apostasy

1. Did no trace of a church remain in Israel then?
*Calvin says it depends. In falling away there are degrees. Under
Rehoboam, the godly had a church in passable condition. Under
Ahab, they did not.*

[9]

A Corrupt Church

1. According to Calvin, is the Roman church better or worse than Israel
under Jeroboam?
Markedly worse.

2. What two things are demanded by the Romanists if Protestants are
to come back into communion with Rome?
*First, participation in all the prayers, sacraments, and ceremonies.
Second, that they grant to the Roman church every privilege and
honor that Christ gives to the church in the Bible.*

3. Did the prophets of the Old Testament set up pure sacrifices during
times of corruption?
*No, they did not. But neither would they participate in idolatrous
worship that was set up to rival what God had established. No
prophet ever worshiped at Bethel.*

[10]

Separation Necessary

1. Why did the prophets separate from certain assemblies?
Because they had become wicked conspiracies against God.

2. What would follow if the Roman churches were still churches?
*They would still have the power of the keys. But the power of the
keys is linked to the word, and they no longer have the word.*

[11]

Vestiges

1. Does Calvin deny everything churchly to the papists?
   No, there are still traces of the church there.

2. What does Calvin mean by "traces"?
   He principally means baptism, but he also acknowledges that there are other vestiges as well.

3. What metaphor does Calvin use?
   It is like a ruined building, not leveled to the ground. When a half-demolished building remains, the outline of it can still be seen.

[12]

Sound Elements

1. Do the remaining sound elements make the corrupted church the true church?
   No. But by saying that Rome is not the church, Calvin is not maintaining that there are not any churches among them.

2. Who, then, is Calvin's chief foe?
   His chief foe is the Roman pontiff, who is the "leader and standard bearer of that wicked and abominable kingdom."

3. What argument does Calvin use to indicate the church is not completely gone there?
   The fact that the pope exalts himself in the Temple of God.

4. What soundness remains in Rome?
   A remnant of God's people are there, woefully scattered, and some marks of the church remain—baptism occupying the first place.

5. What is lacking with every one of their congregations and their whole body?
   The lawful form of the church.

CHAPTER THREE

[1]

Church Order

1. If the Lord alone is to have rule in the church, then why has He established a governmental order?
   So that His will might be revealed to us as a sort of delegated work.

2. What is a useful exercise in humility?
Recognizing the fact that we are to obey God's word, even though it is preached by men like us, and sometimes even by men of lower worth.

3. How may we best evidence our piety and obedience?
By showing ourselves teachable to God's minister, even if he excels us in nothing.

[2]

Significant Ministry

1. What is a "chief sinew" holding the church together?
This human ministry.

2. What is it therefore to argue against this kind of government?
It is to argue for the destruction of the church.

[3]

The Prestige of Preaching Ministry

1. How should we consider the preaching ministry?
As something to be held in the highest honor and esteem, as the most excellent of all things.

2. What was a mode of governance established by the Lord forever?
Governing and keeping the church through ministers.

[4]

Different Sorts of Officers

1. What five offices does Calvin list?
From Ephesians 4:11—apostles, prophets, evangelists, pastors, and then teachers.

2. Which from this list are ordinary?
The last two, pastor and teacher.

3. When are the other offices discharged?
At the beginning of the kingdom, and every now and then as circumstances demand.

4. What was the task of the apostle?
To lay the foundation of the gospel in all the world.

5. What was the function of the prophet?
To excel in a particular revelation.

6. Does Calvin believe the office of prophet has ceased?
For the most part.

7. What was the function of an evangelist?
That of functioning in the place of the apostles, although occupying a lesser rank.

8. Were apostles (or at least evangelists) reestablished in the time of the Reformation?
Yes, according to Calvin.

9. What offices are perpetual and exist in all duly ordered churches?
Pastors and teachers.

[5]

Temporary and Permanent

1. If teachers correspond to the ancient prophets, what do pastors correspond to?
They correspond to the apostles.

[6]

Apostles and Prophets

1. What should the heirs of the apostles do?
They should preach the gospel and administer the sacraments.

2. How should men regard ministers?
As ministers of Christ and stewards of the mysteries of God.

3. Why are ministers not set over the church?
In order to get paid.

4. Why are they set over the church?
To instruct the people in true godliness, administer the sacred mysteries, and to maintain discipline.

5. In what should pastors imitate the apostles?
What the apostles did for the world, pastors should do for their own flocks.

[7]

Focus

1. What is each pastor assigned to?
His own church.

2. Does this mean he cannot help elsewhere?
No, he can help.

3. What should he remember as he does?
He should be content with his own limits and not break into another man's territory.

[8]
Interchangeable Terms

1. What terms for the ministry does Calvin use interchangeably?
Bishops, presbyters, pastors, and ministers.
2. What other office functions in the local church?
Men called "governors" (1 Cor. 12:28).
3. What do they do?
They are charged with the censure of morals and the exercise of discipline alongside the bishops.
4. Should all churches have these men?
Yes, every church should have a senate of godly, grave, and holy men. This office is for all ages.

[9]
Deacons

1. How many grades of "deacon" were there?
Two. One distributes the alms, and the other is devoted to the care of the poor and sick.
2. Who occupies this second office?
The women mentioned in 1 Timothy 5:9–10. According to Calvin, women could fill no other public office than caring for the poor.

[10]
An Orderly Call

1. What things should be done "decently and in order" in the church?
All things should be done that way.
2. Are some things more important than others in this regard?
Yes, order is more important in government than anywhere else.

[11]
The Outer Call

1. What aspect of a man's call to the ministry is Calvin treating?
His outward call to the ministry.

2. Why does he pass over the inner call?
Because that is between him and God.

3. Is the outer call lawful even if a man being ordained has an evil conscience?
Yes, provided the wickedness is not known.

[12]

Qualifications for Ministry

1. What sort of man should be chosen to be a minister?
A man of sound doctrine and holy life.

2. What does the church owe such men before ordaining them?
The church owes them training.

[13]

Apostolic Selection

1. Why does the selection of apostles not provide us with a pattern for selecting ministers?
Because with the apostles, the hand of God needed to be more visibly seen.

[14]

Human Agency

1. Did God choose apostles in a way that excluded the church entirely?
No, the church was still included in the process.

[15]

Congregational Voting

1. What does Calvin deny to Titus and Timothy?
An autocratic position in the church.

2. How were presbyters selected (Acts 14:23)?
By a show of hands.

3. What is a lawful call?
When those who appear to be fit are chosen by the consent and approval of the people, with other pastors presiding.

[16]
Ordination

1. Is there a direct command to lay on hands in an ordination?
   No, but the example of the apostles indicates that we should.
2. What does this remind the one being ordained of?
   That he is no longer a law to himself.
3. Who lays hands on the new pastor, according to Calvin?
   Other pastors.

CHAPTER FOUR

[1]
The Ancient Church

1. How has Calvin discussed church government up to this point?
   On the basis of "God's pure word."
2. To what aspect of the discussion does he now turn?
   To the practice of the ancient church before the papacy.
3. What is his conclusion?
   That despite some minor problems with terminology, there was "almost nothing" that was contrary to the Scriptures.

[2]
The Office of Bishop

1. What were all teachers in the ancient church called?
   They were called presbyters.
2. What did the college of presbyters in each city do?
   They chose a man they named bishop, one who would preside over them.
3. Why did they do this?
   Because equality of rank tends to breed dissension.
4. Was this of divine appointment?
   No, it was a human arrangement and was recognized as such.
5. Who was the first to adopt this arrangement?
   The evangelist Mark was elected as the first bishop of Alexandria.
6. What was the position of the bishop with regard to the other presbyters?
   He was above them in dignity but still subject to them.

[3]

The Duties of Bishops

1. What was the central duty of both presbyters and bishops?
   The dispensing of word and sacraments.

2. What happened by Gregory's time?
   The church had deteriorated much from its ancient purity.

3. But what was still true at that time?
   The duty of a bishop to preach, though somewhat neglected, was still recognized.

[4]

Other Ranks

1. What did each province have?
   An archbishop over the bishops.

2. What happened at the Council of Nicea?
   Patriarchs were ordained to be higher in rank and dignity than archbishops.

3. Why does Calvin object to the word *hierarchy?*
   Because it leads to men lording it over other men in government.

4. What does he not object to?
   Some men having greater dignity. But he objects to this translating into an authority that is unaccountable.

5. What is his summary of the ancient church?
   That they did not intend to fashion a church rule other than that laid down in God's word.

[5]

Deacons

1. What were the responsibilities of deacons in the early years?
   To feed the ministers and to feed the poor.

2. What was the bishop's responsibility?
   To identify which of the poor should receive the deacons' help.

3. How is the deacons' office toward the poor described?
   Under the bishop, they were stewards of the poor.

4. Where did archdeacons come from?
   When the financial responsibilities got more complicated, they held the office of "treasurer" or "trustee."

[6]

Patrimony

1. What were the church's possessions considered to be?
   As the patrimony of the poor.

[7]

Fourfold Division

1. Why were certain canons formed?
   Because of the misbehavior of a few.

2. What were the four divisions of the church's revenue?
   They were for the clergy, for the poor, for the upkeep of buildings, and for the bishop's hospitality.

[8]

Financial Balance

1. Did the early church maintain balance between care of buildings and care of the poor?
   Yes, and Calvin cites examples.

[9]

Other Offices

1. How did Calvin understand the other offices that developed?
   As not being offices proper, but rather being occasions for training young men for office.

[10]

Consent of the People

1. What ancient practice in the government of the church does Calvin commend?
   The requirement that church officers be chosen by the consent of the people.

2. When a church was afflicted with an evil presbyter, did they have a remedy?
   Yes, there were many canons to deal with such things.

[11]

More Consent

1. If a bishop chose his own successor, what was then required to ratify it?
   The consent of the people.

[12]

Not Commended

1. Did Calvin believe that the people needed any restraint or discipline in this?
   Yes. Their right to choose their leaders in the church did not mean they had the right to riot or raise a tumult.

2. Does Calvin approve any mechanisms to restrain the people in this?
   Yes, but only so long as their voice is still heard and honored.

[13]

Church Elections and Emperors

1. How long did the old method of selecting church rulers last?
   At least to the time of Gregory, and probably after.

2. When was the last election of the pope ratified by the consent of the people?
   Just five hundred years before Calvin.

3. What cities required the emperor's consent before a bishop was installed?
   Rome and Constantinople, the two imperial capitals.

[14]

Ordination

1. What did the Latins call the act of setting apart a church officer?
   They called it ordination or consecration.

2. What did the Greeks call it?
   Raising of hands.

3. What had to accompany ordination?
   An examination.

[15]

Laying On of Hands

1. Why did men start going to the metropolitan to be ordained?
   Because of ambition and the deterioration of the old order.

2. How was the ordination accomplished?
Through the laying on of hands.

3. In those days, what was the only difference between a bishop and a presbyter?
The presbyter could do everything a bishop could do except ordain.

—————— CHAPTER FIVE ——————

[1]

Learning

1. Is hierarchy important to the Roman church?
Yes, they are always talking about it.

2. If they ordain a man of learning, what is he likely to know?
He is likely to be a lawyer who knows how to plead in court, but not how to preach in a church.

3. What sorts of men are ordained?
Dissolute men, not to mention mere boys.

[2]

A Lost Franchise

1. What has vanished from the church?
The right of the people to vote for their bishops.

2. When bishops are presented to the people, what is it for?
So that they might be adored, not examined.

3. What should you do if the medicine has become more deadly than the disease?
It should be remedied—but they won't.

[3]

The Princes Intrude

1. What is wicked spoliation?
To force upon the people a bishop they have not desired or approved of freely.

[4]

What Accompanies Ordination

1. What should accompany ordination?
   A charge to exercise the office.

2. According to the Roman masters, what should be taken care of in religion?
   The belly.

[5]

Shameless Laughter

1. When the worth of worthless candidates is expressed during ordination, what are they doing?
   They are shamelessly laughing at God and men.

2. Why are they willing to act against anyone who speaks openly against their sacrilege?
   Calvin answers this with a question. Would they act this way if they thought there was a God?

[6]

Benefices

1. What stipend or living used to be connected to ordination?
   A benefice, but that was no longer the case in Calvin's day.

2. Under the papacy, how are most benefices secured?
   With some form of simony.

[7]

Monstrous Abuses

1. What kind of man is given rule in five or six churches?
   The kind of man who cannot rule himself.

2. Why is it useless to cite the word against these people?
   Because the word has long ceased to matter to them.

3. What is maintained, as they claim, by this villainy?
   The church is kept from perishing by their villainy.

[8]

Two Kinds of Priest

1. What are the two kinds of priests in the Romanist system?
   Priests and seculars.

2. What is Calvin's take on this division?
   He maintains that monks cannot discharge the pastoral office, and so they should not have it. The seculars, by implication, should fulfill that office.

[9]

Privilege

1. How are benefices apportioned?
   By privilege or custom without reference to the word of God. Calvin wants the system overthrown.

[10]

Outward and Inward

1. What sort of abuse is Calvin not addressing?
   Various outward abuses. He is focusing on the inward evil rooted in this system.

2. What have these men thrown off?
   Preaching, discipline, and the administering of the sacraments.

[11]

Two Legitimate Offices

1. What two offices does Calvin allow as excellent, provided they are fulfilled?
   The offices of bishop and parish rector.

[12]

The Time of Gregory

1. What is a failing as early as the time of Gregory?
   Priests not teaching enough. And if Gregory complained about this neglect, what would he say about the conditions of Calvin's time?

[13]

Apostolic Pretensions

1. When the bishops claim to have a succession from the apostles, what does Calvin ask?

What do they have in common with the apostles?

[14]

Lifestyle

1. What is this order of men notorious for?

For excess, effeminacy, and voluptuousness.

2. If the bishops and priests were judged by the canons of the early church, what would happen?

They would be deposed from office or excommunicated.

[15]

Alms

1. What do the deacons no longer do, a task essential to their office?

They no longer distribute alms.

[16]

The Canons

1. According to the canons, what portion of the church's income should go to the poor?

At least a fourth.

[17]

The Prophecies

1. How does Calvin interpret the prophecies of the church's coming splendor?

He interprets them spiritually.

[18]

Raised from the Dead

1. For those who pride themselves on their connection to antiquity, what unanswerable argument does Calvin raise?

   What certain ancient bishops would say if they were raised from the dead and given a tour of the conditions current in Calvin's day.

[19]

Church Order

1. Where is it foolish to seek church order?

   In the midst of these corrupt bishops and abbots.

2. According to Jerome, what was the glory of the bishop?

   To provide for the poor.

3. What was the disgrace of all priests?

   To seek after their own riches.

CHAPTER SIX

[1]

Submission to Rome

1. What is the principle of unity for the Roman church?

   The principle of unity is the head of the earthly church, the pope.

2. How do the Romanists define schism?

   Any separation from that church.

[2]

Aaron and Sons

1. What argument for papal supremacy is made from the Old Testament?

   From the headship of Aaron as high priest.

2. How does Calvin answer this?

   By pointing out that rule over one nation surrounded by idolatry is not comparable to rule over all men, East and West.

[3]

The Word to Peter

1. What is the central argument from the New Testament?
   The promise give to Peter in Matthew 16:18.

[4]

The Power of the Keys

1. How does Calvin take the promise given to Peter?
   As referring to his apostolic authority, given also to the others.
2. How does he show this?
   By pointing to the place later in Matthew (18:18) where it is given to all the apostles.
3. What two early fathers does he cite in favor of this interpretation?
   Cyprian and Augustine.

[5]

Honor Is Not Power

1. What fundamental distinction with regard to leadership does Calvin make in this section?
   The distinction between honor and power. The fact that Peter was honored by the other apostles does not mean that he had power over them.

[6]

One Foundation

1. What does Calvin take as the "rock" upon which Christ will build the church?
   The confession that Peter made, on his own and in the name of the others.

[7]

Peter and the Others

1. What does Peter do after the decision of the Jerusalem council?
   He submits to it, obeying it.
2. What does Paul expressly argue in Galatians?
   That he is not behind any of the other apostles in authority, with Peter expressly named.

[8]

Primacy of Honor

1. What sort of primacy does Calvin grant to Peter?
   A primacy of honor. He was a natural leader among the apostles.

2. What does he do with the illustration of bees and cranes?
   He points out that each group has its own leader, but that all the cranes in the world do not.

3. What does Calvin conclude in the argument about kingdoms?
   That kingdoms cannot have two kings, not that the whole world should be one kingdom.

[9]

Christ the Head

1. What does Calvin call the idea of having the whole world under one earthly head?
   Utterly absurd.

2. Who is the sole Head of the Church?
   Christ.

3. And what is excluded by this?
   The idea of a vicegerent. Life spreads to the whole body directly from the Head.

[10]

An Argument from Silence

1. What place in the New Testament should have argued for the papacy, if there were such an institution?
   The passage in Ephesians 4, where Christ ascended and gave gifts to men.

[11]

Rome Is Not Peter

1. Supposing that Christ gave Peter the supremacy, what does Calvin argue next?
   That this in no way transfers to Rome.

2. What other example did he give?
   Christ was the Bishop, and He did not acquire this honor for Jerusalem.

[12]

What about Antioch?

1. What was Peter's first see?
   Antioch.

2. What does Calvin argue from this?
   That Antioch should have the primacy.

[13]

Other Patriarchates

1. What other question is raised about Antioch?
   If the primacy was transferred to Rome, why wasn't Antioch the second in rank?

2. What patriarchate did take second place?
   Alexandria, and the first bishop there was a mere disciple, not an apostle—John Mark.

3. What patriarchate took last place?
   Jerusalem, which is odd.

[14]

Peter in Rome

1. What is the principle reason Calvin doesn't believe Peter was ever bishop in Rome?
   Not enough time. He was in Jerusalem for twenty, and then Antioch for a while. And late in Paul's life, there is no reference to Peter in Rome.

[15]

Peter and Paul

1. Why does this involve a character issue for Peter?
   Paul says that at the end of his life "all forsook him" (2 Tim. 4:16). If Peter was in Rome, that would include him as well.

2. Does Calvin allow that Peter may have been martyred in Rome?
   Yes, but not that he was bishop there.

3. Why should we focus more on Paul?
   Because we are Gentiles, and Paul's apostolate was for us.

[16]

Three Reasons

1. What were the three reasons Calvin gives for the rise of Rome's importance?

Because of the opinion that Peter had ministered there, because it was the capital city and many gifted men were there, and because Westerners are not as enamored of novelty as Christians elsewhere, and so Rome was a calmer place, a place of refuge for deposed bishops from elsewhere.

[17]

Fathers on Unity

1. What argument does Calvin present from the fathers?

That early church fathers, strongly urging church unity, did not refer to the papacy as a principle of that unity.

———— CHAPTER SEVEN ————

[1]

Position of the Early Roman See

1. When was the primacy of the Roman see first granted?

At the time of the Council of Nicea.

2. Were the legates of the Roman church given first place at that council?

No, they were granted the fourth place.

[2]

Chalcedon

1. Why was the Roman church given the first seat at Chalcedon?

Because of an extraordinary circumstance. Leo asked for the first place from the emperor because of the earlier misbehavior of the Eastern bishops when they had the first seat.

2. Did Rome have the first seat at subsequent councils?

No. Not at the Fifth Council at Constantinople, for example.

[3]
Proud Titles

1. What does Calvin call titles like "primate"?
A proud title by which Romanists wonderfully vaunt themselves.

2. What does Cyprian do in his dealings with Pope Stephen?
He deals now with his arrogance and now with his ignorance.

3. What does Jerome say about the primacy of one see over the others?
He says that wherever a bishop may be, whether at Rome, or Gubbio, or Constantinople, he has the same merit and same priesthood as elsewhere.

[4]
Gregory's Rejection

1. What title did Gregory reject for the bishop of Constantinople?
The title of universal bishop.

2. Did he reject it for others because he wanted it for himself?
No, it was an unacceptable title for anyone.

3. Such a title was precursor to what?
It was a precursor to the Antichrist.

4. According to Gregory, how does the title "universal bishop" threaten the Church?
Because the universal Church would fall if that bishop did.

[5]
The Origin of the Problem

1. How long does Calvin believe Rome has sought to have lordship over other churches?
There was no time when they weren't trying something or other.

2. What happened when Athanasius was unjustly deposed from his see?
He came to Rome for support.

3. Why was this a bad precedent?
Because the Roman bishop continued to receive refugees who had been justly disciplined.

[6]

Church Power

1. What are the four kinds of church power as outlined by Calvin?
   Ordination of bishops, calling of councils, hearing appeals, and issuing chastisements or censures.
2. What did the early behavior of Rome indicate with regard to ordination?
   Fellowship with other churches, not lordship over them.

[7]

Mutual Admonition

1. What do ancient admonitions show us?
   That while the Roman bishop delivered admonitions, he also had to receive them from others.

[8]

Convening Synods

1. Who had the authority to call a universal council?
   The emperor, and not the Roman bishop.
2. What does Calvin not deny with regard to the Roman bishop?
   That he was one of the chief bishops. But he denies him dominion over all.

[9]

Shamelessness

1. What shows the shameless grasping for power that Rome was guilty of?
   Her use of obvious forgeries to advance her claims.

[10]

An Early Snarl

1. What early tangle shows the nature of the Roman bishop's authority?
   The case of Caecilian, who had been condemned by Donatus and had appealed to the emperor.
2. What happened?
   The emperor assigned the case to the bishop of Rome, and when the decision favored Caecilian, the appeal went to the bishop of Arles.

[11]

Forgeries

1. What is characteristic of most of the forgeries giving the Roman pontiff great power?

They are infantile, and just about anybody can see through them.

2. Are all such documents forgeries?

No. Pope Leo was immoderately fond of glory and would make such claims. But that would offend the others of his day.

[12]

The Power of Rome Grows

1. What happened during the time of Gregory I?

The empire was disintegrating, and many churchmen around the Mediterranean would ally themselves with Rome.

[13]

Mutual Submission

1. What kind of authority does Gregory exercise?

The kind of authority that he would be willing to submit to when wielded by others.

2. What is distressing to Gregory?

That he has to be taken up with administration when he wants to discharge the true office of a bishop.

[14]

Struggle for Primacy

1. Why were Rome and Constantinople in a struggle?

They struggled over which bishop should have the primacy.

2. How was the pecking order of the churches established in the first place?

In accordance with the civil order of the Roman empire.

3. What was the older rule when civil primacy was transferred to another city?

The older rule was that ecclesiastical primacy went with it.

4. Which pope altered this rule?

Innocent.

[15]

Leo and Nicea

1. What did Leo try to prevent?
   Constantinople being given the second place.
2. Why?
   Because it was closer to first place.

[16]

Gregory and John

1. Why did Gregory resist John?
   Because he wanted the bishop of Constantinople to be the universal bishop.
2. Was he jealous for the title for himself?
   No, he rebuked Eulogius for using it on him.

[17]

Pepin and Zachary

1. What happened in Gaul?
   When Pepin usurped the kingdom, he and the pope divvied up the spoils like robbers.

[18]

Bernard

1. How does Calvin use the testimony of Bernard?
   To show how corrupted everything had become by Bernard's time.

[19]

Later Papal Claims

1. How do Romanists define the pope?
   As the supreme head of the church on earth, and the universal bishop of the whole world.
2. What do these claims "amount to"?
   They amount to a claim of supreme jurisdiction.
3. For Calvin, what is the most unbearable aspect of this?
   The fact that there is no restraint allowed against potential abuses.

[20]

New Forgeries

1. What is put forward by the forgeries?
   The claim that this is the way it has been from the beginning of the church.

2. What does Calvin say about such claims?
   That they are "wholly groundless."

3. What does he call people who are carried to this point of madness or blindness?
   Antichrists.

4. In addition to supremacy, what other claim is made on behalf of the pope?
   Infallibility.

[21]

Ancient Testimonies to the Contrary

1. What does Cyprian deny?
   That there can be a bishop of bishops, or first bishop, or prince of priests.

2. What does Gregory deny?
   That there can be a universal bishop.

3. What does Gregory say to the bishop of Alexandria?
   That in degree the other bishops are his brothers, and in moral character, his fathers.

[22]

The State of the Papacy

1. How does the papacy of Calvin's day compare to previous ages?
   It is much worse than Gregory's day and a little worse than Bernard's.

2. What are Romanists doing when they appeal to the middle period of Gregory and Leo?
   They are like those who praise the virtues of the Roman republic in defense of the monarchy of the Caesars, borrowing the praises of freedom to adorn their tyranny.

[23]

A Failed Church

1. What kind of church does not exist at Rome, according to Calvin?
   The kind that can have "benefits of this sort"—i.e., the blessings of church government.
2. If something is not a church, what can it not be?
   The mother of churches.
3. Is Calvin speaking of the people?
   No, only of the government.
4. Why does Calvin say the Roman bishop is no bishop?
   Because he doesn't even pretend to discharge the office of a bishop.

[24]

A Bishop or King?

1. How must a bishop's office be ordered?
   It must be ordered according to the words of Christ.
2. Why does Rome persecute the church?
   That is the only way she has to hold on to her power.

[25]

Antichrist

1. How does Calvin defend his use of the term "antichrist"?
   By an appeal to 2 Thessalonians 2:4.

[26]

No See

1. Where can the honor of a see not stand?
   Where there is no see.

[27]

Three Basic Convictions

1. What three basic convictions does Calvin attribute to the pope and college of cardinals?
   First, that there is no God. Second, that the gospels are a false and deceitful set of lies. And third, the doctrine of the resurrection is a mere fable.

2. How does Calvin come to this?
From the shamelessness of the popes.

[28]
John XXII

1. What pope fell openly into error?
John XXII, who asserted that souls are mortal and die along with the body until the day of resurrection.
2. What is affected by this notion?
The doctrine of papal infallibility.

[29]
Papal Immorality

1. How does the parade of immorality at Rome affect the idea that Rome holds the office of bishop?
Men who live like this are anything but bishops.

[30]
Cardinals

1. What does Calvin show concerning the office of cardinal?
That it did not exist in the ancient church and in the middle period was an entirely different office.

——— CHAPTER EIGHT ———

[1]
The Word Sets the Limits

1. What is the only way to build up the church?
It is for the ministers to endeavor to preserve Christ's authority for Himself.
2. What happens when we just grant men the power they are disposed to take?
Tyranny happens.

[2]

Moses and the Priests

1. Is authority given to men personally?
   No, it is invested in the office they hold.
2. What example does Moses set?
   That of speaking nothing but His word.

[3]

Authority of Prophets

1. What were prophets forbidden to do?
   To speak anything of their own.
2. What do they receive when they limit themselves according to the word?
   They are given extraordinary power and excellent titles.

[4]

Authority of Apostles

1. What may apostles not do?
   They may not prate whatever they please.
2. The power of the church is not what therefore?
   It is not infinite but is enclosed within the word.

[5]

Fundamental Revelation

1. God has never revealed Himself to men except through what means?
   Except through His Son.

[6]

Shielded from Novel Doctrines

1. How did God shield His people from novel doctrines?
   By giving them His word as a boundary.

[7]

Last Word

1. How shall we regard the revelation of God in the Son?
   As the final and eternal testimony from Him.

[8]
A Firm Principle

1. What is to be a firm principle?
   That no other word is to be held as the word of God, or treated as such in the church, than what is contained in Scripture.

[9]
Apostles Held Fast

1. Were the apostles free to go beyond the word?
   No, still less their successors.

2. How should pastors be endowed?
   By all things in God's word, including the shepherding of the church within and the rule of the world without.

[10]
Universal Councils

1. What do Calvin's opponents say about universal councils?
   That they are the true image of the church, governed by the Holy Spirit, and that they cannot therefore err.

[11]
What Calvin Grants

1. What does Calvin grant?
   That God governs His people through His Spirit, and that His Spirit is not a spirit of error.

2. But what boundary remains?
   Always the word. The Spirit will not lead His people in ways contrary to His word.

[12]
The Church Not Infallible

1. What is referred to in the passage that says the Church is the pillar and ground of the truth?
   Paul refers to the ministry of preaching.

[13]

Word and Spirit Together

1. Where should the Church set the limit of its own wisdom?
   Where Christ has made an end of speaking.

2. How does the Spirit then lead the Church into all truth?
   By bringing them back to what Christ said.

3. How is the Spirit conjoined with the word?
   With an insoluble bond.

[14]

Tradition

1. Does Calvin allow an infallible oral tradition from the time of the apostles?
   No, not at all.

[15]

No New Coinages

1. What should every sensible man see?
   How perilous it is to give men authority to coin new doctrines apart from the word.

[16]

Infant Baptism

1. Does Calvin allow that infant baptism has no scriptural support?
   No, not at all.

2. What does he call the fathers' use of the term "consubstantial"?
   He describes it rightly as a mere expositional term.

CHAPTER NINE

[1]

Preface on Councils

1. What is Calvin's attitude toward the ancient councils?
   He venerates them from his heart.

2. What does the fact that he thinks less of the councils (formally) than his opponents not mean?

It does not mean that the decisions of those councils support his opponents.

[2]
True and False Councils

1. In order for a council to have spiritual authority, what must it do?

It must gather in Christ's name and do what it does in accordance with the word.

[3]
With or Without Pastors

1. What does Calvin prove from multiple places in the Old Testament?

That pastors and priests can (all of them together) deal falsely.

[4]
A New Testament Concern Also

1. Does this possibility only exist during the time of the Old Testament?

Not at all. Peter warns of it (2 Pet. 2:1), as does Paul (Acts 20:29–30).

[5]
Discernment

1. What does the pope think is necessary in order to be a true council?

Just simply having the name of pastors.

2. How does this conflict with the word of Jeremiah the prophet?

Jeremiah's foes thought the authority of the word could not be separated from them.

[6]
Truth and the Councils

1. How does Calvin handle the reply that while priests can err, councils of priests are protected from error?

By showing that water does not rise above its own level. The council will partake of the nature of those who make it up.

[7]

The Condemnation of Christ

1. By what means was Christ condemned, and why does it matter?
   He was condemned by a church council. And this obviously shows the depth of error that councils can fall into.

[8]

Nicea and Chalcedon

1. Does Calvin have a high view of Nicea and Chalcedon?
   Yes, provided that Scripture stands in the highest place.

2. Did those councils have any problems?
   Yes, they certainly did. So we don't accept them blindfolded.

[9]

Council against Council

1. What were the decisions of Constantinople and Nicea?
   They were, respectively, that images in churches should be destroyed and that they should be established.

2. What about Chalcedon and Ephesus II?
   The Eutychean heresy was embraced at Ephesus and condemned at Chalcedon.

3. What conclusion should we draw?
   That councils generally cannot be trusted straight across.

[10]

The Chief Article

1. What chief article of our faith was upheld by Nicea?
   The deity of Jesus Christ.

[11]

Fallible Councils

1. What did Leo say about Chalcedon?
   He granted it was a legitimate council but still subject to error.

2. What did Gregory of Nazianzus think of councils?
   He thought they always came to a bad end.

[12]
No Blind Obedience

1. How do we know that certain pastors must be heard and others rejected?
   Because of the Scripture passages that tell us to beware of false teachers.

[13]
The True Weight

1. What role then do councils have?
   Their decisions, if based on Scripture, have much greater weight than the determination of individual bishops.

2. What men does Calvin praise?
   Athanasius, Basil, Cyril, and other vindicators of true doctrine, raised up by the Lord.

[14]
The Canon of Scripture

1. What does Calvin say about the view that makes the boundaries of Scripture dependent on councils?
   He says it is a blasphemy unfit to be mentioned.

─────────── CHAPTER TEN ───────────

[1]
Binding the Conscience

1. What do the Roman traditions do?
   They ensnare miserable souls.

2. What is the point under discussion?
   Whether the church may lawfully bind consciences by its laws.

3. What kind of church law does Calvin not contend against?
   He does not argue against useful institutions that help maintain discipline, honesty, and peace.

[2]
Paul's Example

1. Why did Paul deal with this kind of issue so cautiously?
   Because he saw (1 Cor. 7:35) what a wound would be inflicted on consciences if he went beyond what God had imposed.

[3]
What Conscience Is

1. What does conscience not allow a man to suppress?
   His instinctive knowledge of right and wrong.

[4]
A Good Conscience

1. What is a good conscience?
   An inward uprightness of heart.

[5]
Law and Conscience

1. How does the conscience answer to men?
   It doesn't. The conscience answers to God alone.

2. When men frame laws, where do they not apply?
   To the inward governing of the soul.

[6]
No Right to Command

1. What do the bishops have no right to command?
   No right to command as obligatory what they conceived apart from Scripture.

[7]
Lawgivers

1. How many lawgivers does Scripture recognize?
   Just one (Jas. 4:11–12; Is. 33:22).

[8]

Two Reasons

1. What are the two reasons why the Lord claims lawgiving as His right alone?

First, His laws are sufficient for all that we need. Second, He is the only one with authority over our souls.

[9]

Two Areas of Claimed Authority

1. What two areas does Rome claim authority over?

Over the area of ceremonies and over discipline.

[10]

Papal Constitutions

1. What examples does Calvin use to show that the Romanists have developed the same inverted values that Jesus chastised the Pharisees for?

By teaching that it is more wicked to skip annual confession than to live wickedly for the whole year. By teaching that it is worse for a priest to be bound in one lawful marriage than to be caught in a thousand adulteries. By teaching it is worse to defile your body with a taste of meat on Friday than to be polluted with fornication.

[11]

Two Objections

1. What are the two other faults that Calvin finds with the papal constitutions?

First, they are useless and sometimes foolish. Second, there are a multitude of them, impossible to keep.

[12]

Worldly Wisdom

1. What does a man puffed up with worldly wisdom think of the ceremonies?

He is marvelously captivated by ceremonial pomp.

[13]

Senseless Accumulation

1. According to Calvin, where does Paul teach the innate tendency of human traditions to become increasingly burdensome?
   In Colossians 2:20–21. First is the prohibition of eating, then the prohibition of tasting, and after that, a prohibition even to touch.

[14]

Ceremonies and Christ

1. What do these ceremonies do to Christ?
   They half bury Him.

2. How does Calvin answer the objection that the simple people, the uneducated people, need ceremonies?
   By saying that it is not the way to take care of weak people—by overwhelming them with "great heaps of ceremonies."

[15]

Corruption of Ceremonies

1. How does God accept the works of the law which we do?
   They have grace only from God's free kindness.

2. Ceremonies are corrupt and harmless unless what?
   Unless men are led to Christ through them.

3. What is a cunning craftsman?
   The belly.

4. What does Calvin mean by this?
   That men devise ceremonies as a means for priestlings to catch money.

[16]

Multitudes of Ceremonies

1. How do ceremonies obscure the clarity of the gospel?
   By their multitude.

[17]

Adding and Subtracting

1. What is the church universal forbidden to do?
   To add to or take away from anything from God's word when worship or salvation are involved.

[18]

Innovations

1. Does Calvin grant that these customs go back to the time of the apostles?
   No. They don't even go back to the time of the apostolic tradition.

2. How did these ceremonies develop?
   Holy bishops introduced some for order and discipline. They were followed by careless men, who began trying to outdo the previous innovations and to defend their innovations more strictly.

[19]

Useless Rites

1. What are some of the accumulated customs that Calvin objected to?
   Priestly vestments, altar ornaments, gesticulations, and so forth.

[20]

Free Conscience

1. Is Calvin open to certain exercises of extrabiblical piety?
   Yes, so long as the conscience is left free, and no one makes a law to entrap consciences in bondage.

[21]

Acts 15

1. Did the Jerusalem Council establish a new law?
   No. The apostles "instituted or decreed nothing new there."

2. What were they requiring?
   That Christians not offend one another.

[22]

Obligation to Weaker Brethren

1. How does Calvin know that the Jerusalem Council was not fundamentally concerned with the eating of meat sacrificed to idols?
   Because of Paul's teaching elsewhere in 1 Corinthians 8.

[23]
Scripture and Tradition

1. And when Scripture and a particular custom conflict, what must happen?
   The custom must give way.

2. What passage from the gospels does Calvin cite in this regard?
   Matthew 15:9.

[24]
Perverse Worship

1. How does Calvin interpret Paul's prohibition of "will-worship" (Col. 2:4)?
   As sham obedience that requires what God did not require as though He did.

[25]
Old Testament Examples

1. How does Calvin handle the examples of Samuel, Manoah, and Gideon sacrificing in places not prescribed by the law?
   By pointing out that Samuel was not disobeying because God had not yet established a place for worship, that Manoah was acting under inspiration, and that Gideon really was disobeying.

[26]
Moses' Seat

1. What did Christ mean by the command to listen to the Pharisees?
   He meant that their correct teaching was not to be rejected because of their hypocrisy. But He also warned against their false teaching, the leaven of the Pharisees.

2. He quotes Augustine to what effect?
   For those who need authority beyond reasons, he quotes Augustine saying that overseers are divided into two categories, sons and hirelings.

[27]
Necessity of Church Order

1. What mistake do some make in reaction to the Romanists?
   They throw out all constitutions, including those that conduce to good order.

2. Is Calvin against every form of organization?
Not at all. It is necessary for every form of human society.

3. What happens without set forms?
The sinews of that society disintegrate.

[28]

Right Church Constitutions

1. What is the central requirement of proper church constitutions?
That love be fostered among us by common effort.

[29]

True Decorum

1. What does Calvin want to establish in worship instead of trifling pomps?
An arrangement that takes away "confusion, barbarity, obstinacy, turbulence, and dissension."

[30]

Bondage and Freedom

1. What are the two opposite errors when it comes to church constitutions?
One is to impose impious and tyrannical laws. The other is, in reaction, to leave no place at all for holy laws.

2. What is the example that Calvin uses?
That of kneeling.

3. In what sense is this custom divine and in what sense human?
It is divine in that we see it approved in Scripture. It is human in that we must decide how that posture will be incorporated in our services.

4. What is our best and most safe guide?
Love, and a desire to edify the church.

[31]

Other Examples

1. What are some of the other practices that Calvin includes under this heading?
Women without a shawl and burial customs are two.

[32]

Unfortunate Necessity

1. Is every custom that needs to be disposed of an evil custom?
   No, but some ancient practices that were initially edifying have got-
   ten too tangled up with superstitions to be retained.

————— CHAPTER ELEVEN —————

[1]

Power of the Keys

1. What is the next part of ecclesiastical power?
   The power of jurisdiction and discipline.
2. Where does Calvin say the New Testament gives the church the authority to rule?
   In Romans 12:8; 1 Corinthians 12:28; and 1 Timothy 5:17.
3. What does this authority rest upon?
   The power of the keys given by Christ.

[2]

Binding and Loosing

1. What distinction does Calvin make between the binding and loosing
   of Matthew 16 and 18?
   It is the same authority, he says, but the former expressed through
   preaching and the latter through discipline.

[3]

Different Sorts of Jurisdiction

1. What distinguishes civil from ecclesiastical authority?
   The church does not have the authority of coercion, which the state
   does.
2. What will happen to a drunk or a fornicator in a well-ordered city?
   He will be punished.
3. What should happen if he grumbles about it, not repenting.
   The church deals with him by holding him back from the Supper.

[4]

Priest and King

1. What is not fitting?
   For the church to accuse to the magistrate those who do not obey the church's admonitions.

2. Where is a good emperor?
   Within the church, not over the church.

[5]

The Aim of Discipline

1. What is the aim of ecclesiastical discipline?
   That offenses be resisted and scandals addressed.

2. What two things must be taken into account?
   First, that this spiritual power be completely separated from the power of the sword, and second, that discipline be the decision of a plurality.

[6]

Ancient Elders

1. What limits did Cyprian put on his authority?
   He determined not to do anything in his bishopric without the consent of the clergy and of the people.

2. In the ancient church, in the senate of the presbyters, what were the two kinds of elders?
   Those who had been ordained to teach, and those who were simply to be censors of morals.

[7]

Deterioration

1. What evil has arisen from the church getting involved in earthly matters?
   The tribunal of the church has become a brawling court.

2. What sorts of offenses are addressed?
   The debts of poor men.

3. And what are not addressed?
   The corrupt lifestyle of others, priests included.

[8]

Opulence and Proud Titles

1. Why did the Romanists believe the pope had the power of the sword?
   Because it was not exercised over consciences.

2. What did they think constituted a mutilation of their authority?
   Failure to deck the order out with opulence and proud titles.

3. What did Ambrose say about the separation of these governments?
   "To the emperor belong the palaces; to the priest the churches."

[9]

Bishops or Princes?

1. What does Calvin call the assumption of the power of the sword by bishops?
   He calls it "that shamelessness."

2. Where did the Lord prohibit such power to the church?
   In Matthew 20:25–26.

[10]

How It Happened

1. How did bishops gain this power?
   By various means over the centuries. They acquired the power by trickery, by the misguided generosity of princes, the turning of voluntary arbitration into legal jurisdiction, and times when people sought protection from their bishops because of a particular crisis.

2. But what would they do if they had any spark of the apostolic spirit?
   They would abandon temporal power, citing Paul's words in 1 Corinthians 10:4.

[11]

Bernard's View

1. What did Bernard say that Peter left to his successors?
   He gave the care of the churches.

2. What do bishops have instead of a scepter?
   A hoe.

[12]

Donation of Constantine

1. What does Calvin call the Donation of Constantine?
   Fraudulent and absurd.

[13]

When the Pope Seized Power

1. When does Calvin hold that the pope attained power over princes?
   Five hundred years before, in the time of Hildebrand.
2. Why did this happen?
   Because the princes were weak and cowardly.

[14]

Instruments

1. What three instruments do the popes use to attain these ends?
   Fraud, treachery, and war.

[15]

Immunities

1. In ancient times, in what sense were the clergy under the authority of the prince?
   In matters pertaining to the church, they were not. In matters pertaining to the civil order, they were.

[16]

Maintaining Order

1. In what sense were the bishops subject to the princes?
   When the princes were preserving the order of the church and not disrupting it.

——— CHAPTER TWELVE ———

[1]

Church Discipline

1. What does discipline depend upon?
   Upon the power of the keys and spiritual jurisdiction.
2. What are the two kinds of discipline?
   The kind to which clergy and laity alike submit, and the kind that pertains to clergy alone.
3. What are the sinews that hold the body of Christ together?
   Discipline.

[2]

Private Admonition

1. What is the first stage of church discipline?
   Private admonition.
2. Where does it end?
   Publicly, before the tribunal of elders.

[3]

Hidden and Open Sins

1. What are the two kinds of sins with regard to public knowledge?
   Some are private or hidden, while others are known to all.

[4]

Light and Grave

1. What is another division that can be made between sins?
   Some are merely faults, while others are crimes or shameful acts.

[5]

Three Reasons

1. What is the first reason for church discipline?
   To keep the name "Christian" held in honor, and to keep from profaning the Lord's Supper.

2. What is the second?
The second is to prevent the corruption from spreading in the body.

3. What is the third?
The restoration of the offender.

[6]

Practice of Discipline

1. What are the two kinds of sins that church must address?
Public sins and private sins with witnesses.

2. What kind of sin does the church not address?
Hypocritical private sin with no witnesses.

3. How does the church handle scandalous public sins?
By instant discipline; the steps of Matthew 18 are not necessary.

[7]

Princes and Citizens Alike

1. Who is subject to discipline?
Everyone. Princes are not exempt, as witnessed by the example of Theodosius.

2. Do the elders take action in isolation?
No. They must act with the knowledge and approval of the whole church.

3. Why is this necessary?
To prevent tyranny from developing. It is so that nothing will be done according to the whim of a few.

[8]

A Chief Fault of the Ancients

1. What aspect of church discipline in the early church is Calvin critical of?
Their undue severity.

[9]

Limits of Love

1. What should temper our discipline?
Our love for the offender (2 Cor. 2:8).

[10]

Excommunication as a Corrective

1. What are the two ways of putting a man away from the church?
   Excommunication and anathema.

2. What is the difference?
   Excommunication seeks the repentance of the offender. Anathema writes him off.

3. How often is anathema used?
   Seldom, if ever.

4. Why must gentleness be maintained in censures?
   To keep discipline from sliding down into butchery.

[11]

An Early Witness

1. Which church father does Calvin cite in defense of this position?
   Augustine against the Donatists.

[12]

Dealing with Rigorists

1. What group contemporary with Calvin resembled the ancient Donatists?
   The Anabaptists, who recognized no assembly unless it was characterized by an angelic perfection.

2. Do such men really hate other men's wickedness?
   Not so much as they love their contentions.

[13]

Levels of Discipline

1. According to Augustine, when is the "severe mercy" of sharp discipline necessary?
   When the contagion of sin invades the multitude.

[14]

Another Form of Discipline

1. What other element of discipline, not properly contained within the power of the keys, is important?
   The discipline of fasting.

2. What sort of occasion would call for this?
When dealing with a judgment from the Lord or on an important occasion, like the selection of a minister.

[15]

Three Objectives

1. What are the three objectives of fasting?
To weaken and subdue the flesh, to prepare for prayers and holy meditations, and to abase ourselves before the Lord in the confession of guilt.

2. Which of these is public and which private?
The first is private, and the last two are both public and private.

[16]

Fasting in Itself

1. Are fasts (including sexual fasts) an end in themselves?
No, they are of no importance except as they are connected to their purpose or point.

[17]

Averting God's Wrath

1. What is the hope in public fasts in the face of calamity?
That God would stay His hand.

2. Do we need to do this less than the ancients did?
Not at all—we face calamities just as they did.

[18]

A Tempered Life

1. What should the life of the godly be like overall?
Tempered with frugality and sobriety.

2. Does Calvin allow for modified fasts?
Yes, as when someone eats plainer foods, and less of it, in order to concentrate on prayer.

[19]

Superstitious Fasting

1. What are the three dangers that Calvin mentions with regard to fasting?
Thinking that external conformity is sufficient, thinking that it is a meritorious work, and thinking of it more highly than we should.

[20]

Christ and Fasting

1. How many times is it recorded that Christ fasted?
Only once, at the beginning of His ministry.

2. Why did He fast?
To demonstrate the continuity of His ministry with that of Moses.

[21]

Corrupt Fasting

1. How had the Romanists corrupted fasting?
By refraining from meats in order to gorge on various other delicacies.

[22]

Clerical Restrictions

1. In ancient times, what was prohibited to the clergy by the canons?
Things like hunting, gambling, reveling, wanton dances, and the like.

2. Who had to live more strictly, the clergy or laity?
The clergy, which Calvin approved.

3. What does Calvin point out about the practice of the Romanists of his day?
That their behavior had no connection to the ancient practices.

[23]

Celibacy

1. In what area is Rome strict?
In the prohibition of marriage.

2. But what do they not prohibit at the same time and with the same zeal?
Fornication. That vice prevails among them unpunished. If a priest takes a wife, he is punished, but not if he takes a whore.

3. On what basis does Calvin object?
On the basis of Scripture. Man must not bind what God has left free.

[24]

Marriage Enjoined

1. How do the Romanists interpret Paul's requirement that a bishop must be married?
By saying that it means that a man with two wives is disqualified.

2. What do their canons call cohabitation?
Uncleanness and pollution of the flesh.

[25]

Levite and Christian

1. According to Calvin, how are Levite priests and Christian pastors distinct?
The Levites were antitypes of Christ, and this is why they refrained from sexual activity in the course of their duties.

2. What was the example of the apostles?
They kept wives and traveled with them (1 Cor. 9:5).

[26]

Celibacy

1. Why did contentions at Nicea arise when some tried to advance celibacy?
Because there are always "superstitious little fellows."

2. What recommendation from Paphnutius was actually adopted?
The statement that lawful cohabitation was a form of chastity.

[27]

Gradual Developments

1. How did celibacy as a priestly requirement begin?
It began with a too great admiration of celibacy and moved on to frequent and unrestrained rhapsodic praises of virginity. This meant that married men were treated as though they had no interest in aspiring to Christian perfection.

[28]

New Tyranny

1. If the Romanists want to follow the practices of antiquity, what does Calvin say they should do first?
Restore discipline for adultery and fornication.

2. If they did that, would Calvin be content?
No, he says that the requirement of celibacy is bondage.

3. What does Chrysostom, an admirer of virginity, say about the married state?
That the first degree of chastity is sincere virginity, the second faithful marriage.

———— CHAPTER THIRTEEN ————

[1]

Degeneration

1. What is the entire praise of righteousness?
Simple obedience to what God has revealed.

2. What is the difference between a promise and a vow?
A promise is to men and a vow to God.

3. What do we promise men?
What we think will please them, or what we owe them.

4. How does this apply to vows?
We should think of them the same way.

[2]

Three Things

1. What are the three things to keep in mind concerning vows?
First, to whom the vow is made; second, who we are in making the vow; and third, what our intention is.

2. Why is the nature of God important?
He declares all self-made religion detestable to Him, and so our vows ought not to be part of a self-made religion.

[3]

Considering Our Own Frame

1. What two things must we remember in considering our own condition?
We must know our own strength, and we must know our own calling.

2. What does Calvin call vows of celibacy here?
Something that holds the first place for insane boldness.

3. What do people who take these vows rashly discover?
That celibacy is one thing, virginity another.

[4]
Motive and Intention

1. How does intention figure into vows?
If a man vows to abstain from wine as though that were good in itself, then he is superstitious. If he has a noble purpose, then he is not.

2. What two sorts of vows have reference to the past?
Vows of thanksgiving, and vows of repentance.

3. Are both lawful according to Calvin?
Yes.

[5]
Vows for the Future

1. Does Calvin allow for vows to restrain future behavior?
Yes, but within limits.

2. What limits?
They must be supported by God's approval, agree with the man's calling, and be within his capacity.

[6]
Basic Vows

1. What is the basic vow of a Christian?
Baptism.

2. How is this vow confirmed and sanctioned?
Through catechism and the Lord's Supper.

3. Does this vow anticipate the presence of sin?
Yes, forgiveness of sins is part of the covenant of grace.

4. Beyond this, what does Calvin require of particular vows?
That they be sober and temporary.

[7]
Perverse Vows

1. When men vow to abstain from good things willy-nilly, what does Calvin call that?
They are vows full of manifest impiety.

[8]
Ancient Monasticism

1. What was ancient monasticism for?
   It was sort of a "boot camp" to prepare men for ministry.

2. Does Calvin allow that it was the same institution as in his day?
   No, not at all.

[9]
Augustine's Description

1. What was the severity of monasticism tempered by in Augustine's day?
   It was tempered by brotherly love.

[10]
Early and Late Monasticism

1. What is the chief part of the sanctity for the monks of Calvin's day?
   Idleness.

2. According to Augustine, what was almost the only rule for monks?
   Brotherly love.

[11]
Striving for Perfection

1. What kind of life do monks think they live?
   A perfect life.

2. When pressed, what dodge do they fall back on?
   That they, alone among men, are striving for perfection.

[12]
The Advice of Christ?

1. Do monks shoulder a greater responsibility for obeying Jesus?
   They think so.

2. What did the ancient fathers teach about this?
   That all men must obey every little word uttered by Christ.

[13]
If You Would Be Perfect

1. When Jesus told the rich young ruler to sell all his goods if he would be "perfect," what was He doing?
   The young man had a secret wound, and Christ was probing it.

2. Was He commending voluntary poverty as a way of life?
   No. It was as though an ambitious man was told to give up his honors, etc.

[14]
Monastic Sectarianism

1. What does Calvin call blasphemy?
   The idea that monastic vows are a second baptism.

2. How were the ancient monks different from Calvin's contemporaries?
   They stayed part of the general church, while Calvin's contemporaries withdrew.

3. What does Calvin call this?
   Sectarianism. He says that every monastery is a "conventicle of schismatics."

[15]
Indictment of the Monks

1. What is rare among monasteries?
   Finding one that is not a brothel.

2. Even in Augustine's day, what does he lament?
   Even when the best can be found in monasteries, it was also true that the worst were there.

3. Does Calvin think there were any good monks left?
   Just a handful.

[16]
Critiquing the Ancients

1. Does Calvin have anything to say that is negative about the ancient monks?
   Yes. While defending them against the charge that they were as corrupt as his contemporaries, he also says the ancients were not without immoderate affectation and perverse zeal.

[17]

Whatever They Vow

1. What does Calvin think of monkish vows?
   Because they are trying to accrue merit, whatever they vow is abominable in God's sight.

2. What must a monk who is gifted with continence be able to do?
   His mind as well as his body must be unsullied by lust.

3. What should a monk do if he cannot keep his vow?
   He should take a wife.

4. What twisted logic by the Romanists does Calvin reject?
   The idea that it would be worse to take a wife sexually than to be guilty of fornication.

[18]

The Case of Enrolled Widows

1. What argument do the Romanists make from 1 Timothy 5:12?
   That vows of celibacy were customary under the apostles.

2. What does Calvin grant?
   That such vows were made.

3. What does he deny?
   He denies that the end of the vow was not something inherently religious, but rather something that enabled the widows to perform their new duties for the church.

4. What three points does Calvin make about this?
   First, that celibacy was not vowed for its own sake. Second, that they were not so bound by the vow that marriage was closed off for good, provided they were having trouble containing themselves. And third, that Paul set an age limit that made such accommodation very unlikely.

[19]

Nuns Are Different

1. What does Calvin call these enrolled widows?
   Deaconesses.

2. What does Calvin call the vows of nuns?
   This "cursed halter."

3. What is the principal difference between the vows of nuns and the vows of widows/deaconesses?
The age at which they are taken.

[20]

Binding Vows

1. Are monastic vows binding?
Not at all, Calvin says.

2. What is his reasoning?
That if the vows are worthless to God, then they should be worthless to us.

3. What does God forbid?
The taking of such vows and continuance in them.

[21]

Breaking Vows

1. Where has there been no bond?
Where God abrogates.

2. What relation does all this have to the Jewish law?
If God set His people free from Torah, how much more will He set them free from these man-made laws?

3. What is characteristic of almost all monasteries?
They swarm with impurity.

─────── CHAPTER FOURTEEN ───────

[1]

Definition of a Sacrament

1. What does a sacrament do?
It is an aid to our faith related to the preaching of the gospel.

2. How does Calvin define a sacrament?
He says it is an outward sign whereby the Lord seals on our consciences the promises of the gospel in order to strengthen us in our weakness, and whereby we attest our piety before the Lord, angels, and men.

3. What is Augustine's shorter definition?
A visible form of an invisible grace.

[2]
Sacrament and Mystery

1. The Latin word "sacrament" translates what Greek word?
   Musterion, *or mystery.*

[3]
Hidden and Open Sins

1. What are the two kinds of sins with regard to public knowledge?
   Some are private or hidden, while others are known to all.

[4]
What the Word Does

1. What does the word that accompanies the sacrament do?
   It explains what the visible sign means.

2. Does the mere speaking of the word do anything?
   Not according to Augustine. The word is spoken so that the hearers (and recipients of the sacrament) would believe it.

3. What does the sacrament require in order to beget real faith?
   It requires preaching.

[5]
Sacraments and Seals

1. How do we know that sacraments are seals?
   Because Paul calls circumcision a seal (Rom. 4:11).

2. How does a believer use the sacrament?
   He does not halt at the visible sight of them but rather ascends by devout contemplation to the hidden mysteries contained within.

[6]
Signs of the Covenant

1. What relation does a sacrament have to the covenant?
   It is a token or sign of it.

2. What else does Calvin call the sacraments?
   He says they are pillars of our faith.

[7]
Heavier Condemnation

1. When the wicked come to the sacraments, does this mean those sacraments are not testimonies of God's grace?
   No. Those who abuse God's grace in this way receive heavier condemnation because they are abusing grace.

2. If the wicked could undo God's grace this way, what effect would this have elsewhere?
   It would mean that neither gospel nor Christ would be testimonies of God's grace either.

3. How does Paul speak of the sacraments when addressing believers?
   He includes in them the communication of Christ—e.g., Galatians. 3:27 and 1 Corinthians 12:12–13.

4. How does he speak of them when unbelievers are in view?
   As cold and empty figures.

[8]
Confirmation through the Sacraments

1. What are we if we grow old without advancement?
   Thrice miserable Christians.

2. What three essential things does God do for us?
   First, He teaches us through His word. Second, He confirms it by the sacraments. And third, He illumines our minds to both word and sacrament by means of His Holy Spirit.

[9]
Sacraments the Spirit's Tools

1. Do the sacraments work by themselves?
   No, they are tools the Spirit uses.

2. When do sacraments fulfill their office?
   Only when the Holy Spirit uses them.

3. Where does the power rest, and where does the ministry lie?
   The power rests with the Spirit, the ministry with the sacraments.

[10]

Preparation and Confirmation

1. What work does the Spirit do to prepare us for the sacraments?
   He softens the heart and composes it for the obedience it must render to the word of the Lord.

2. What work does He perform to make it efficacious to our souls?
   He transmits the outward words and sacraments from our ears to our soul.

[11]

Word and Sacrament

1. What two things work equally to confirm our faith?
   Word and sacrament.

2. What does the Lord compare the Word to?
   To a seed, which can be fruitless or fruitful, depending on how it is received.

[12]

Tree of Life as Sacrament

1. What does God sometimes do when He would remove confidence in the reality of salvation?
   He sometimes takes away the sign of it, as He took the tree of life from Adam.

2. What does Calvin say to those who object that this take on the sacraments diminishes God's glory?
   He says that God routinely works through means, and there is no reason it should diminish His glory.

[13]

A Military Oath

1. What does Calvin say to those who held that *sacramentum* referred to the oath a soldier took?
   He denies the relevance of this. He says the early Christians appropriated a term for their own use and assigned their own meaning to it.

2. Who is he reasoning against here?
   The Zwinglians.

[14]
Holding Forth Christ

1. By minimizing the sacraments this way, what do these men do?
They completely overthrow the use of it.

2. How does Calvin categorize the opposite error?
He says it is diabolical.

3. What is that error?
That the sacraments justify and confer grace, provided we do not commit mortal sin.

4. What is the certain ruin of the church?
Receiving the sacraments without faith.

5. What does the promise of the sacrament include?
Wrath for unbelief.

[15]
Sacramental Essence

1. According to Augustine, what must be distinguished?
The sacrament and the substance of the sacrament.

2. In our understanding of the sacramental union, what must we continue to distinguish?
The matter from the sign, lest we transfer to the one what belongs to the other.

3. In the elect, what do the sacraments do?
They effect what they represent.

4. What was the sacrament to Judas?
It was poison, not because he received an evil thing but because he received it in sin.

5. What must we do as we eat with our mouths?
We must chew with our hearts as well.

[16]
Faith and More Faith

1. What must the sacraments have in order to promise anything?
They must have all their firmness in and through Christ.

2. Does receiving the sacrament carnally make the sacrament less spiritual?
No, it just makes it unspiritual for the unworthy partaker.

3. According to Augustine, what are the two vices to be avoided?
   To receive the sacraments as though they don't do any good, and to receive the sacrament while not lifting our minds beyond the visible sign.

[17]

A Settled Principle

1. What should be a settled principle with regard to sacraments?
   That they have the same office as the Word of God, which is to offer and set forth Christ.
2. Under what conditions are sacraments spiritually useless?
   When they are not received in faith.
3. Is God present in the institution?
   Yes, by the power of His Spirit.
4. How do sacraments work?
   God accomplishes within what the minister represents without.

[18]

Sacraments in a Wider Sense

1. In the history of God's people, what are the two kinds of sacrament that God has used?
   The natural and the miraculous.
2. What are some examples of the former?
   The tree of life and the rainbow.
3. What are some examples of the latter?
   Abraham's smoking fire pot, Gideon's fleece, and Hezekiah's sundial.

[19]

Sacraments Now

1. What are sacraments from God's side?
   They are testimonies of His grace and salvation.
2. What are they on our end?
   Oaths of allegiance, whereby we bind ourselves to Him.

[20]

The Promise of Christ

1. Why did the sacraments vary in the time of the Old Testament?
   They varied with the times.

2. What were some Levitical sacraments?
   Purification and sacrifices.

3. How many ordinary sacraments do we have now that Christ has come?
   Two—baptism and the Lord's Supper.

4. Would Calvin be willing to call anything else a sacrament?
   Yes, but not an ordinary sacrament—e.g., the laying on of hands in ordination.

[21]

Looking Forward to Christ

1. What was the meaning of circumcision?
   That all fleshly seed was corrupt and in need of pruning.

[22]

Fully Expressed

1. What is different about the sacraments in the new covenant?
   Christ is more fully expressed in them.

2. What did Augustine call the blood and water that came from Christ's side?
   The wellspring of the sacraments.

[23]

Shared Reality

1. Though Christ is more fully expressed in our sacraments, is He more fully present in them?
   No, not at all. The believers in the Old Testament shared the same reality that we do.

2. What does Paul do to warn the Corinthians by the example of the Jews in the wilderness?
   He makes the Jews equal to us in sacraments.

3. What did the Jews receive in their sacraments?
   Christ with His spiritual riches.

[24]

Value of Circumcision

1. Do New Testament statements disparaging circumcision reduce that sacrament far below baptism?
   Not at all, because if there is no faith we should say the same things about baptism.

2. What is the relationship of circumcision to baptism?
   What it was for the ancients, baptism is for us.

[25]

Empty Ceremonies

1. How does Calvin explain the apostolic disparagement of Mosaic ceremonies?
   By showing that it was spoken in controversy, against those who were trusting in them falsely.

2. When does Calvin approve such ceremonies?
   When they are taken in their true and natural sense, and not when they are perverted.

[26]

Some Overstatement

1. Does Calvin complain about some of Augustine's language?
   Yes, saying that it is exaggerated, but not disagreeing with Augustine's point.

2. What did Augustine mean in comparing the Mosaic to the Christian sacraments?
   He said that the Mosaic law foretold Christ, while ours set forth Christ.

3. But what is the constant between the two?
   Christ is the constant.

CHAPTER FIFTEEN

[1]

Baptism and Forgiveness

1. What are we received into by means of baptism?
   The society of the Church.

2. What are we supposed to understand from our baptism?
   It is a token and proof of our cleansing.

3. Is baptism a mere token or mark?
   No. We are to receive baptism as connected to the promise of salvation.

[2]

Virtue in the Water

1. Why does baptism keep us from trusting in mere water?
   Because baptism states that Christ's blood is our true and only laver.

2. What does baptism, rightly understood, help us to fasten our minds upon?
   Upon Christ alone.

[3]

All Sins

1. What sins are cleansed by means of a right use of baptism?
   All sins throughout our whole life.

2. Do sins committed after baptism negate that baptism?
   No, not at all.

3. What do men gather for themselves if they try to abuse this grace?
   They provoke nothing but wrath and judgment.

[4]

Water and Blood

1. What does the power of the keys depend upon?
   It depends on baptism.

2. What is linked together therefore?
   Preaching the word, baptism, and the power of the keys.

[5]

Baptism and Renewal

1. How is baptism made a true blessing?
   It is made a true blessing by right faith.

[6]

A Trinitarian Work

1. What do the different Persons of the Trinity do in our salvation?
   The Father is the cause, the Son the matter, and the Spirit the effect of our purgation and regeneration.

[7]

John's Baptism

1. Does Calvin make any fundamental distinction between John's baptism and Christian baptism?
   No, he says they are essentially the same.

[8]

The President of Baptism

1. Who presides over baptism, regardless of who administers it?
   Christ alone presides.

[9]

Our Exodus

1. Who is drowned in our baptism?
   Our Pharaoh, that is the devil.

[10]

Original Sin

1. For Calvin, does baptism eradicate original sin?
   No, but rather deals with the condemnation of it.
2. Does Calvin believe that infants are sinful?
   Yes. They have not yet sinned themselves, but they have the seed of sin enclosed within themselves.
3. How may we have righteousness in this life?
   By imputation only.

[11]

Struggle against Sin

1. Is lust ever completely eradicated in this life?
   No. We are freed so that it might not overcome us, but it is never completely gone.

2. Should this make us careless in our fight against sin?
   No. We should constantly struggle manfully against sin, have courage for the way, and spur ourselves on to final victory.

[12]

The Romans 7 Struggle

1. How does Calvin interpret the struggle in Romans 7?
   As the internal struggles of the regenerate soul.

[13]

A Token of Allegiance

1. What other purpose does baptism serve?
   It serves as a confession of allegiance before men.

[14]

Surest Rule

1. What is the surest rule of the sacraments?
   That we should see spiritual things in the physical.

2. If we have faith, do we have mere appearance only?
   No. God leads to the reality, and the sacraments effectively perform what they symbolize.

[15]

Not Weakening

1. Is it Calvin's intent to weaken the force of water baptism?
   No, not at all.

2. What is the glue that joins the reality to the sign?
   Faith, and faith only.

[16]
The Worth of the Administrator

1. What illustration does Calvin use to show baptism is not nullified by the unworthiness of the man who administers it?

If the handwriting and seal of a letter are recognized, the character of the postman doesn't matter.

[17]
Delayed Repentance

1. Does Calvin grant that he and others had been long in unbelief after their baptisms?

Yes, but the fault was theirs. There was no fault in the promise contained in the baptism.

[18]
Rebaptism

1. If the baptism of John was true baptism, then how does Calvin handle the baptism again of those who had been baptized before (Acts 19)?

He denies that they were baptized (in water) again. He says it was the baptism of the Spirit, given through the laying on of hands.

[19]
Alien Hodgepodge

1. What does Calvin think of baptismal "extras" like chrism, exsufflation, and the like?

He calls them an alien hodgepodge.

2. What should we omit from baptismal ceremonies?

All theatrical pomp.

3. What does Calvin say about the mode of baptism?

That it doesn't matter and should be allowed to vary according to the usage of different countries.

4. Nevertheless, what does he say the word "baptize" means?

He says that it means to immerse and that the ancient churches practiced it this way.

[20]

Baptism by Laymen

1. Does Calvin believe that laymen should baptize in emergencies?
   No, because he points out that it is not an emergency. It would only be an emergency if salvation were dependent upon it.

2. Do we baptize infants to bring them into the promise of salvation?
   No. We baptize them because they are already encompassed in the covenant of salvation.

[21]

Baptism by Women

1. What does Calvin think about baptisms performed by women?
   He is against it entirely, no exceptions.

[22]

Zipporah's Example

1. What does Calvin do with the example of Zipporah circumcising her son?
   He says it is actually an example of a usurpation and a bad attitude.

—————— CHAPTER SIXTEEN ——————

[1]

The Attack on Infant Baptism

1. Who attacks infant baptism, according to Calvin?
   Certain frantic spirits.

2. What is the appearance of their argument?
   It is seemingly quite plausible.

3. And what is it?
   It is that infant baptism is not founded on any institution of God.

[2]

The Meaning of Baptism

1. What should we not focus on in baptism?
   We should not focus on appearances, but rather raise it to God's promises.

2. Are we to reason from baptism to the promises, or the other way?
   The other way.

[3]

Baptism and Circumcision

1. To what in the Old Testament does Calvin compare and contrast baptism?
   Circumcision.

[4]

Differences

1. What are the differences between circumcision and baptism limited to?
   They are limited to externals only.

[5]

Infants in the Covenant

1. Are infants participants in the life of the covenant?
   Yes.

2. What does Calvin infer from this?
   That if they participate in the thing signified, why should they be driven away from the figure?

[6]

Christ in His Coming

1. What did Christ not do in His coming?
   He did not truncate or curtail the grace of God.

2. What are the children of at least one Christian?
   Holy, and not unclean like the children of idolaters.

3. If infant baptism is successfully denied, what would this do to Christ's coming?
   It would mean that Christ came to make God's grace more obscure and less available.

[7]
Blessing the Children

1. Why did the Anabaptists not accept Christ's blessing of the children as a reason for baptizing them?
Because blessing, not baptism, is mentioned.

2. How does Calvin answer this?
By pointing out the reason for the blessing. Christ blesses them because "of such" is the kingdom of heaven. If children can possess the reality, then why not the sign?

[8]
Argument from Silence

1. If we accepted that infant baptism is unbiblical because it is not mentioned, then what else is unbiblical?
Admitting women to the Lord's Supper.

[9]
Baptism and Circumcision

1. If someone fires a jest at infant baptism, what else do they hit?
Circumcision, which is unquestionably of divine origin.

[10]
Beasts or Men?

1. In order to sharply distinguish circumcision and baptism, what do the Anabaptists do?
They divide the two covenants, and to such an extent that they portray the Jews as being extremely carnal, more beasts than men.

2. And if that were the case, what were the benefits like that God gave to them?
Like the food that a herd of swine receive.

[11]
Colossians 2:11

1. What was Paul's point in Colossians 2:11?
He was teaching that baptism is for the Christians what circumcision was for the Jews.

2. What does Calvin call the doctrine that the Old Testament signs were merely earthly and literal?
He calls it selling smoke.

[12]
Stopping Too Soon

1. What is the sin of these "fickle spirits"?
It is that they stop their studies too soon instead of comparing many things together.

2. What are they gravely mistaken in?
In thinking that God's spiritual blessings were never promised to Abraham's physical offspring.

[13]
Father Abraham

1. How are both circumcision and uncircumcision made equal in honor?
Abraham was both, so that he could be the father of both kinds of men who believe.

2. Why do Gentiles who believe not have to be circumcised?
They have baptism in place of it.

3. Why does Paul deny that Abraham is father of the circumcision alone?
To crush the pride of those who preen themselves on ceremonies alone.

[14]
Physical Descent

1. Does Calvin make physical descent from Abraham nothing?
No. He simply insists that there is no reason to boast in the covenant unless they keep the law of the covenant, which is to obey the word genuinely.

[15]
No Allegorical Fulfillment

1. With regard to the relationship of physical and spiritual realities, is the condition of Christians different from that of the Jews or the same?
It is exactly the same.

[16]

Men and Women

1. What does Calvin do with the argument that women ought not to be baptized if they were not circumcised?
It is a reductio, *and he dismisses it. He says that it is plain that Jewish women were included in the Old Testament rite, although not by direct participation.*

[17]

Old Enough to Be Born Again

1. What do Calvin's opponents conclude about the parentage of children?
That they should be considered as children of Adam until they are old enough to be born again.

2. Does Calvin agree that they are in Adam?
Yes.

3. And what does he say should happen?
They should be brought to Christ, who is life.

4. How does he reply to those who object that infants cannot be regenerated?
He points to the example of John the Baptist (Lk. 1:15).

[18]

Christ Sanctified

1. Why was Christ sanctified from earliest infancy?
So that He might sanctify in Himself His elect from every age group without distinction.

[19]

Infants Knowing the Gospel

1. What does Calvin say about the capacity of infants to know the gospel?
He allows that they may not experience faith the same way we do, but this does not mean that they cannot experience a tiny spark of it.

[20]

Infants Cannot Repent

1. What does he do with the objection that infants cannot repent?
   Calvin points out that infants were circumcised, and circumcision was a sign of repentance.
2. What are infants baptized into?
   Future repentance and faith.

[21]

Buried with Christ

1. When Paul says that we are buried with Christ in baptism, according to Calvin, does he mean that we must be buried with Christ prior to baptism?
   No, he is simply teaching the doctrine that underlies baptism.
2. Where do opponents of infant baptism consistently go wrong?
   By saying that the reality must always precede the thing that signifies it.

[22]

Body of Christ

1. What is Calvin's argument with regard to the possibility of salvation for infants and children?
   If they can possess the reality, then why would we deprive them of the sign?

[23]

False Applications

1. What false application does Calvin reject in this section?
   The notion that we should apply to infants all standards that we would apply to adults who were to be baptized.

[24]

Abraham and Son

1. What does the example of Abraham and Isaac show us about the chronological order of reality and sign?
   With Abraham, the reality came first. With Isaac, the sign came first.

[25]

Water and Spirit

1. How does Calvin understand the phrase "water and Spirit" in John 3?
   As the "Spirit, who is water."

[26]

Saved and Unbaptized

1. Does Calvin believe that remaining unbaptized is no big deal?
   No, he doesn't tolerate it at all. He says that baptism must not be despised.

2. Is baptism necessary to salvation?
   No, and that is his point. While it is a big problem to despise baptism, baptism and salvation are not so annexed as that salvation is impossible without baptism.

[27]

Christ's Baptismal Words

1. What is the next argument Calvin answers?
   The argument that the order of Christ's words specifies the order in which things must be done.

2. How does Calvin answer it?
   He simply says that there is no reason for their inference, and he goes on to provide a counterexample.

[28]

Infants Not Everywhere

1. Does Calvin believe that infants are included in Mark 16:16?
   No, not at all. He says there is not one syllable about infants in the whole discourse.

[29]

Jesus the Prototype

1. Why did Jesus take His baptism when He did?
   He was baptized at the beginning of His ministry. He began His teaching by setting an example of baptism for us.

2. How does Calvin illustrate the fallacy of saying that infants cannot perform the prerequisites assigned to baptism?

By pointing out that the apostle says that if someone is not willing to work, he shouldn't eat (2 Thes. 3:10). Should we starve infants then?

[30]

Baptism and the Supper

1. Does Calvin acknowledge that paedocommunion was common in the ancient church?

Yes, as is clear in Augustine and Cyprian. But he says that the custom fell into disuse deservedly.

2. On what basis does Calvin reject paedocommunion?

Because Paul requests communicants to examine themselves (1 Cor. 11:28).

3. What is his answer to the Passover example?

He claims that the Passover meal was only given to those old enough to inquire into its meaning (Exod. 12:26).

[31]

Answering Servetus

1. What does Calvin devote the next section to?

He spends it answering a series of arguments from Servetus, a man he calls the "great glory of that tribe" of heretics.

2. Although he answers these arguments briefly, what does he call them?

A heap of trifles.

[32]

Gratitude

1. What should our response be to the fact that God has included our children together with us?

Gratitude.

2. When we recognize that God takes and acknowledges our children as His children, what does this motivate us to do?

We are motivated to instruct them in an earnest fear of God and observance of the law.

3. What should we do if we do not wish to obscure God's goodness?

We should offer our infants to Him, seeing that they are members of the church.

—— CHAPTER SEVENTEEN ——

[1]

The Supper

1. What do the signs of wine and bread represent for us?
   The invisible food that we receive from the flesh and blood of Christ.

2. In the Supper, what is God doing for the regeneration of baptism?
   He is preserving and sustaining it.

[2]

Special Fruit

1. What is the special fruit of the Supper?
   Union with Christ.

2. What does it mean that Christ has become son of man with us?
   It means that we become sons of God with Him.

[3]

The Entire Force

1. The entire force of the Supper lies in what words?
   In "which is given for you" and "which is shed for you."

[4]

Meaning of Promise

1. What is not the chief function of the Supper?
   Simply to extend to us the body of Christ.

2. What is it rather intended to do?
   To seal and confirm the promise to us.

[5]

Partakers by Faith

1. What is more clear than the gospel preached?
   The gospel set forth in the Supper and received by faith.

2. What two faults must we guard against?
   Against divorcing the sign from the reality, and secondly, extolling them immoderately to the point where we obscure the mysteries themselves.

3. Do we receive Jesus by mere knowledge?
No. We receive Him by faith as we respond to His promise in the Supper.

[6]
Two Fathers

1. What two fathers does Calvin appeal to as teaching the right relation of faith to the Supper?
Augustine and Chrysostom.

[7]
A Great Mystery

1. Does Calvin believe that he understands the Supper fully?
No. He believes his understanding is true, but the sublimity of the mystery overwhelms him.

[8]
Christ in Us

1. What did we lose because we were estranged from God?
We lost participation in life.

2. Does God quicken our souls only?
No. He also quickens our flesh.

[9]
Heavenly Life

1. What is necessary for us to aspire to heavenly life?
Communion in Christ's flesh and blood.

2. What is the great mystery that Paul refers to?
Being members of His body, of His flesh, and of His bones.

3. What would be extreme madness?
Not to recognize the communion of believers with the flesh and blood of the Lord.

[10]
Christ's Presence

1. In the Lord's Supper, what feeds our souls?
The flesh and blood of Christ.

2. How can Christ's flesh, at such a great distance from us, penetrate to us?
   By the agency of the Holy Spirit.

3. Who alone receives this with benefit?
   Believers only.

4. What should believers be persuaded of?
   That whenever they see the signs, the truth signified is also present there.

[11]

Blessed Effects

1. What does Calvin understand the effects of the Supper to be?
   For the believer, redemption, righteousness, sanctification, eternal life, and all other benefits that Christ gives.

[12]

Spatial Presence

1. Although Calvin affirms the real presence of Christ in the Supper, what kind of presence does he deny?
   Local presence.

2. What does Calvin say is utterly unlawful?
   To draw Christ's body back under corruptible elements or to imagine that His body is present everywhere.

3. How then do we partake of Christ's flesh?
   We do so by means of the Holy Spirit.

[13]

Bread for God

1. Bottom line, what is the affirmation of the Schoolmen?
   That what was previously bread is now Christ.

[14]

Transubstantiation

1. Is transubstantiation an ancient error?
   No. Calvin says it was devised "not so long ago."

2. The Supper visibly witnesses to what?
   It witnesses visibly to the promise in John 6.

3. What must represent spiritual bread?
   Visible bread.

[15]

The Basis of Transubstantiation

1. What was the cause of the "crude imagination" involved in the doctrine of transubstantiation?
    Thinking that consecration was equivalent to a magical incantation.
2. The bread is a sacrament only to whom?
    Only those to whom the word is directed.

[16]

Ascending and Descending

1. What mistake do those make who say the body of Christ descends to the bread?
    They do not understand that God is actually lifting us up to Himself.

[17]

The Supper before the Resurrection

1. What question does Calvin ask that stumps these speculations?
    He asks what Christ offered to His disciples in the Supper the night He was betrayed.

[18]

The Presence Known

1. When is the presence of Christ known?
    When our minds are lifted up to heaven.
2. What logical problem is caused by transubstantiation?
    It separates the body from the blood, if the cup is the blood and the separate bread is the body.
3. How does Christ feed us with the communion of His body?
    Through the power of the Spirit.

[19]

Two Essential Things

1. What are the two essential things that must be maintained in the Supper?
    That there be no detraction from Christ's heavenly glory, and that nothing inappropriate to human nature be ascribed to His body.

[20]
Words of Institution

1. What does Calvin grant is the most plausible objection to his position?
That he departs from the words Christ used when He established the Supper.

2. What does Calvin point out about the use of words like his?
That wooden literalism is not how anybody uses words like this.

3. What is Calvin not trying to diminish?
He is not trying to diminish anything of the communication of Christ's body.

[21]
A Figure of Speech

1. Does Calvin say that "this is my body" is a metaphor?
No, he does not.

2. What figure of speech does he call it?
He calls it metonymy, speaking of a part in terms of the whole.

3. What other example does he use of this?
The place where the rock in the wilderness was called Christ. That did not mean a miracle of transubstantiation, in which the rock was turned into Christ.

[22]
The Word "Is"

1. What part of this argument do his opponents rest most heavily upon?
The force of the word "is" in the phrase "this is my body."

2. How does Calvin answer?
With a cluster of counterexamples—he uses "is" the way it is found throughout Scripture.

[23]
Literalism

1. What problems would result from this kind of literalism?
Calvin points out a lot of difficulties, giving ground to the Anthropomorphites among them. They crudely said that God had a physical body because of certain expressions in Scripture.

[24]

The Limits of Reason

1. What do Calvin's opponents accuse him of?
   They accuse him of limiting God according to the dictates of human reason.
2. How does Calvin reply?
   He points out that his view of the Supper is just as "miraculous."

[25]

Appeal to Power

1. What happens when the transubstantionists run themselves into absurdities?
   They appeal to God's omnipotence as trump card.

[26]

The Body in Heaven

1. What is not Calvin's reason for teaching that the body of Christ is finite in heaven?
   Not because of Aristotle, but rather because of the teaching of the Spirit.
2. What are the three ways, according to Augustine, that Christ is still present among us?
   In majesty, in providence, and in His ineffable grace. Under grace Calvin includes the Supper, provided His presence occurs by the power of the Holy Spirit.

[27]

The Meaning of the Ascension

1. What did the Sophists teach about the ascension?
   That Christ never left earth but became invisible.
2. What does Calvin counter with?
   The reality of the ascension into heaven.

[28]

Testimony from Augustine

1. What do these men appeal to in support of their doctrine?
   To the ancient fathers, even Augustine.

2. What does Calvin answer concerning Augustine?
   That this contention is "absurd." Augustine taught that Christ came down through the sacrament of His body.

3. According to Augustine, why did Christ withdraw His physical presence?
   In order to be with them in His spiritual presence.

[29]

A Lutheran Error

1. What error of Servetus is adopted in order to make it possible for Christ's body to be everywhere?
   Christ's body is swallowed up by His divinity.

2. What is Calvin's central objection to this notion?
   That you can't take away bodily attributes and still have a body.

3. How does Calvin explain Stephen and Paul seeing Christ?
   By saying that they were enabled to see into heaven, and not that Christ came down again bodily.

[30]

Ubiquity of the Body

1. What does Calvin call the notion of the ubiquity of Christ's body?
   He calls it monstrous.

2. What ancient error does this replicate?
   The error of Eutyches.

3. What orthodox understanding of the Incarnation does Calvin hold fast to?
   The understanding that says the union of two natures in the one person of Christ did not confound those natures or mingle them.

4. What distinction from the Schoolmen is Calvin willing to adopt?
   The understanding that when the whole Christ is present, this does not mean He is present in His wholeness.

[31]

Not Brought Down

1. Are we fed by Christ's body through Him coming down from heaven in any way?
   No. Rather, we are lifted up to heaven by the power of the Spirit.

[32]

A Secret Too Lofty

1. Does Calvin claim to comprehend this mystery?
   No. He says it is too lofty for his mind to comprehend or his words to declare.

2. What teaching does Calvin emphatically reject?
   The notion of a mixture of Christ's flesh with our soul.

[33]

What Unbelievers Receive

1. What do inquisitive men demand?
   An exaggerated mode of presence.

2. What is the bond of our union with Christ?
   The secret power of the Spirit, which he earlier calls incomprehensible.

3. Do unbelievers receive the body and blood of Christ?
   No. Although God does offer it to them, their unbelief prohibits a spiritual reception.

[34]

Unbelief at the Supper

1. According to Calvin's opponents, what do the wicked receive in the Supper?
   The body and blood of the Lord.

2. Which church father does Calvin cite in opposition to this?
   Augustine.

3. Where alone, according to Augustine, do the sacraments effect what they symbolize?
   In the elect only.

[35]

Perverted Rashness

1. What has perverted rashness wound up teaching concerning the elements in the Supper?
   That they are worthy of adoration.

[36]

Superstition and Idolatry

1. What is it therefore unsafe to do?
   To wander away from God's simple word.

2. What ought men to do instead of adoring the sacramental elements?
   They ought to adore Him in His heavenly glory.

[37]

Superstition

1. Once it has passed the bounds, what does superstition do?
   It makes no end of sinning.

2. Why should we not adore that concerning which Jesus said, "This is My body"?
   Because Jesus said to eat it, not adore it.

[38]

Mutual Love

1. How does bread represent unity?
   It is made out of a multitude of grains coming together.

2. When we disagree with our brother, what are we doing?
   Disagreeing with Christ.

3. When we love Christ, what must we do?
   We must love Him in His brethren.

[39]

The Need for the Word

1. What must always accompany the sacrament?
   The preaching of the word.

2. What is the minister not addressing?
   He is not speaking to the bread, as though uttering a magical incantation.

3. To whom is he speaking?
   He is speaking to the people.

4. What does silence involve?
   It involves abuse and fault.

[40]

Unworthy Partaking

1. If someone comes to the Supper unworthily, what does it turn into for him?
   Deadly poison.

2. What do wholesome elements do when they enter a corrupted soul?
   They cast it down to greater ruin.

3. Is sacrilege therefore possible at the Supper?
   Yes. Men who profane the Supper by partaking in unbelief are guilty of the body and blood of the Lord.

[41]

Worthy Partaking

1. How did the Romanists interpret worthy participation?
   As being pure and purged of all sin.

2. What did Calvin think that would mean for us?
   He said it would mean we were undone; only despair and deadly ruin would remain.

[42]

Faith and Love

1. How did the Roman approach deprive sinners?
   By its immoderate harshness.

2. What does worthy participation consist of chiefly?
   It consists chiefly in faith, which reposes all things in Christ.

[43]

Trifles

1. What sorts of issues does Calvin say make no real difference in the Supper?
   Whether they return the cup or pass it on, whether they divide the bread among themselves, whether the bread is leavened or unleavened—that sort of thing.

2. How often should the Supper be celebrated, according to Calvin?
   At least weekly.

[44]
Frequent Celebration

1. What was the unvarying rule for the ancient church?
   That no meeting of the church should occur without the word, prayers, partaking of the Supper, and almsgiving.

[45]
Not a Spectator Event

1. What two early fathers objected strongly to the practice of coming to church and not partaking of the Supper?
   Augustine and Chrysostom.

[46]
Annual Partaking

1. What does Calvin call the custom of partaking annually?
   He calls it a veritable invention of the devil.

2. Does he blame Zephyrinus, who instituted it?
   No. He assumes that Zephyrinus was pushing the other way, trying to ensure that Christians communicated.

3. How often should the Lord's Table be set?
   At least once a week for the assembly of Christians.

[47]
In One Kind

1. What does Calvin think of offering the bread only to the communicants?
   He says that it steals or snatches half the Supper from the greater part of God's people.

[48]
Dealing with Arguments

1. What is Calvin's first argument against this?
   He asks where in Scripture the administrators of the Supper are called "sacrificers," which could entitle them to be the only ones who had the cup.

2. What is his second argument?
He asks why Christians partook in both kinds for a thousand years after the apostles.

[49]
Obvious Truths

1. What does Calvin not want to do?
He doesn't want to argue over something so obvious.

2. What does he call Gregory?
The last bishop of Rome.

[50]
More Argument

1. What is Calvin's third argument?
That Christ said of the bread that they should eat, but of the cup He said they should all drink.

2. What is Calvin's fourth argument?
That if the Lord had limited the cup to "sacrificers" only, what man would dared to have altered that?

3. What is Calvin's fifth argument?
That Paul included the cup in what he said he had delivered to the Corinthians.

———— CHAPTER EIGHTEEN ————

[1]
Sacrilege

1. Is the sacrifice of the Mass a profanation of the Supper?
Yes, but more than that it is also a nullification of the Supper.

2. Why is it this?
Because of the belief that the Mass is a sacrifice and an offering to obtain forgiveness of sins.

3. What does this do to the sacrifice of Christ on the cross?
It buries and oppresses His cross.

[2]

The Immortal Priest

1. What does the immortality of Christ mean?
   It means He needs no vicars to replace Him.

2. What do men on earth, acting the role of priests in the Supper, do to the honor of Christ?
   They try to cast Him down from the right hand of the Father, where He remains an eternal priest.

[3]

Table or Altar

1. What happens as soon as an altar is set up?
   The cross of Christ is overthrown.

2. What Scriptures does Calvin appeal to?
   The book of Hebrews, where Christ is said to have been sacrificed once for all, and the Lord's last words on the cross: "It is finished."

[4]

Language of Sacrifice

1. How does Calvin handle the argument that the prophets spoke of the new covenant era in terms of "sacrificing"?
   By pointing out how common it was and showing that the language was typological, just as the old forms themselves were.

[5]

Bloodless or Bloody?

1. What other negative effect does the Mass have?
   It drives the death of Christ from the memory of men.

2. How does it do this?
   By means of countless deaths it creates countless testaments of those deaths, which just confuse the whole point.

3. How does Calvin answer the claim that he is slandering the Catholics, who say that "this sacrifice is without blood"?
   By saying that sacrifices don't change their nature at man's whim. Without shedding of blood there is no cleansing. And besides, what sense does it make to say that the wine turns into blood and yet is bloodless?

[6]

Robbed of Benefit

1. The Mass says that we are redeemed by Christ on what condition?
   On the condition that we redeem ourselves.

[7]

A Great Divide

1. How great a divide is there between the Mass and the sacrament of the Supper?
   As great a divide as there is between giving and receiving.

[8]

Private Masses

1. What is the point of sharing the Lord's Supper?
   The point is to share, which negates the practice of having a private mass.

2. What other fragmentation occurred?
   Innumerable masses were driven into every corner of the church, dragging the people hither and thither, instead of bringing them all together as should have been done.

[9]

The Mass Not Primitive

1. Is there any such use of the Supper in the ancient church?
   Not at all. Calvin says the "whole of antiquity" is against the Romanists.

2. What must the Mass-doctors do?
   On the strength of Hebrews 5:4–5, they must show God as the author of their priesthood or confess that the honor is not from God.

[10]

Detached Sentences

1. How can support for the Mass be found in the ancient authors?
   By means of detached sentences.

2. What do the ancient writers do?
   They use the word "sacrifice," but they mean a sacrifice of praise and thanksgiving.

[11]

A Small Fault

1. Although Calvin praises the early fathers warmly for keeping the right balance, he does criticize them for one thing. What was that?

He says that the way they celebrated the Supper contained an appearance of repetition or renewal. He complains about their anagogical or mystical interpretation.

[12]

Not an Altar

1. What has God given us, and what has He not given us in the Supper?

He has given us a table, not an altar.

[13]

Two Kinds

1. There are two kinds of sacrifice. What are they?

Calvin points out there are sacrifices to express gratitude and praise, and sacrifices to deal with guilt.

2. What does he call them?

A sacrifice of praise or thanksgiving, and a sacrifice of propitiation or expiation.

[14]

Done for Money

1. What outrage is added to the doctrinal blasphemies of the Mass?

The fact that the Mass is sold to particular individuals.

[15]

Plato's Ridicule

1. What practice does Plato mock?

The practice of offering sacrifices to the gods in order to hide sin, with the view to increase one's opportunities for sin.

[16]

Under Thanksgiving

1. What comes under the head of the sacrifices of thanksgiving?

All the duties of love.

2. What is meant by "reasonable worship" in Romans 12?
   Paul is contrasting the sacrifice there with the carnal sacrifices of the Old Testament.

[17]

Sacrifices of Praise

1. How does Calvin demonstrate that it is legitimate to understand "sacrifice" as an offering of praise?
   By means of multiple citations from the Old Testament— for example, Psalm 141:2; Hosea 14:2; and Hebrews 13:15.
2. Where do we lay our gifts?
   On the altar, who is Christ.

[18]

Filth in a Golden Cup

1. What does Calvin compare the abomination of the Mass to?
   To Helen of Troy.
2. What does the Mass swarm with?
   Every sort of impiety, blasphemy, idolatry, and sacrilege.

[19]

Two Sacraments

1. What is the difference between the two sacraments?
   One is for entry into the church, while the other is continual food for the church.
2. What must be annexed to every sacrament?
   A promise of salvation.
3. What follows from this?
   That because men cannot promise salvation, they cannot invent sacraments.

[20]

Sacramental Contentment

1. What should we be content with?
   These two sacraments.
2. Did the Jews have changing sacraments?
   Yes, as with the water from the rock or the bronze serpent.

3. Why did Calvin believe God told us we were in the last days?
   *So that no one would delude himself into thinking he had a new
   doctrine or revelation.*

4. How necessary is the word?
   Without it, even sacraments are not sacraments.

——— CHAPTER NINETEEN ———

[1]
Not a Word Game

1. Who ordains the establishment of sacraments?
   The Lord ordains them.

2. Is Calvin simply contending over names?
   *Not at all—in the case of sacraments the issue is the substance of
   the issue, not the words.*

3. What authority does Calvin grant to Christians?
   *He says they are lords of words and all things—provided a pious
   sense be kept.*

[2]
Divine Authority

1. Who alone can establish a sacrament?
   God alone can establish a sacrament.

2. What does a sacrament do?
   It seals a promise or covenant from God.

3. What must come first?
   The word of God must precede the sacrament.

[3]
The Number Seven

1. What does Calvin find among the church fathers?
   No reference to the number seven.

2. What does Augustine refer to several times?
   *How few in number the sacraments are, then listing baptism and
   the Supper only.*

[4]
Baptized Children

1. Where did baptized children sit in the early church?
   With the catechumens.

2. Does Calvin approve the laying on of hands in confirmation, or in acceptance of someone baptized by heretics?
   Yes, provided it is seen as a blessing only and not a sacrament.

[5]
The First Law

1. What is missing from the "beautifully and charmingly done" confirmation service, considered as a sacrament?
   The word of God is missing.

2. What is the first law of a minister?
   To do nothing without a command.

[6]
Laying on of Hands

1. Why must the Holy Spirit still be present in the Church today?
   Because the Church cannot stand unless He is the guide and protector.

2. Why does Calvin say that the Romanists' laying on of hands is not the same as the apostolic practice?
   Because it is toward "a wholly different end."

[7]
Anointing with Oil

1. What is Calvin's central objection to their use of the "oil of salvation"?
   He asks who taught them to do this. Where is the word?

[8]
What Wickedness

1. What relation of baptism to confirmation does Calvin call "wicked"?
   The idea that baptism has to be completed by confirmation.

2. What ancient council does he cite in support of his view?
   The Council of Milevis.

[9]
Confirmed for Salvation

1. What is Calvin's objection to the notion that confirmation is necessary to make someone a Christian?
   He cannot find the idea in Scripture at all.

[10]
On Par with Donatists

1. In what way do those who put confirmation ahead of baptism compare to the ancient Donatists?
   They think that the worthiness of the minister affects the sacramental action.

[11]
Less than Dung

1. What trivial argument does Calvin dismiss?
   The argument that oil goes on the forehead in confirmation while water in baptism goes on the head.
2. What value does Calvin place on this oil?
   Less than one piece of dung.

[12]
Value from Ancient Times

1. How does Calvin answer the argument that confirmation was practiced in the ancient church?
   He says even if that is true, it does not deal with the issue because sacraments are of heaven, not of earth.
2. What else does he do?
   He goes on to show that the ancient church did not practice confirmation as a sacrament.
3. How did they use the "laying on of hands"?
   To receive repentant heretics back into the fold.

[13]
True Confirmation

1. What would Calvin like to see instituted as a "true confirmation"?
   Catechizing children or preadolescents. His example is a child of ten.

[14]
A Rite of Penance

1. What rite of penance would Calvin accept?
   A ceremony to receive heretics back, as the early church had, provided it was understood to be a ceremony prescribed by men and not by God.

[15]
Penance No Sacrament

1. What is Calvin's restatement of his definition of a sacrament?
   An outward ceremony instituted by God to confirm our faith.

2. What advantage should we gain from a sacrament?
   We should ascend from sensible signs to that which is spiritually understood.

[16]
Why Not Absolution?

1. How does Calvin "kill these beasts in their own arena"?
   By showing that on their principles, absolution should be the sacrament, not penance.

[17]
Return to Baptism

1. What is the sacrament of repentance?
   Baptism.

2. What should someone do who has sinned after his baptism?
   He should recall his baptism, bringing it to mind.

[18]
The Third False Sacrament

1. What is the third false sacrament?
   After Calvin treats confirmation and penance, he comes to extreme unction.

2. What do we gain from the Lord's pattern in healing?
   We observe how much freedom He used in His methods.

3. What was the oil for in James 5:14?

It was a symbol so that the unschooled might learn the source of healing power—with oil representing the Holy Spirit.

[19]
Healing Today

1. Does the Lord heal today?

Yes, no less frequently "than of old," but not through these "manifest powers."

[20]
Fails the Test

1. What two things must a sacrament have, according to Calvin?

God's institution and God's promise.

[21]
On Their Own Terms

1. But granting that James 5:14 is a sacrament, what does Calvin point out?

That the Romanists don't do what James requires, in multiple respects.

[22]
Clerical Orders

1. What does Calvin point out about the sacrament of holy orders?

That it is very fruitful and must of necessity divide into "seven sacramentlings."

2. Do their writers agree on how many clerical offices there are?

No, the answers vary.

[23]
Christ and Seven Offices

1. What is Calvin's response to the claim that Christ occupied all seven offices, thus sanctifying them?

He laughs at it as trifling and absurd.

[24]
Lower Offices

1. What is another problem with the lower offices?
   Those who hold them do not discharge them.

[25]
The Tonsure

1. What is the central problem with tracing the tonsure to 1 Peter 2:9?
   That it applies a text that is speaking of all believers to a select few.
2. What is another problem with describing this group as holy?
   There is no class of men more "greedy, stupid, and lustful."

[26]
No Nazarite Vow

1. How does Calvin answer the claim that Paul took the tonsure (Acts 18:18)?
   In two ways. By saying that it shows the Judaizing tendency of the Romanists, and secondly, by showing that Paul was deferring to weaker brothers and not trying to sanctify himself.

[27]
History of the Tonsure

1. What was the origin of the tonsure?
   The clergy was originally ordered to shave their heads to distinguish themselves from effeminate men.

[28]
All of Us Priests

1. Does Calvin affirm the priesthood of all believers here?
   Yes. We offer up praises and thanksgiving, and we do so as priests.
2. Why is ordination not a sacrament?
   Because it is not ordinary or common with all believers.

[29]

Ceremony of Ordination

1. Why does Calvin not accept the appeal to the Lord's example of breathing on the disciples?

Because other things the Lord did are not also imitated, such as His command to Lazarus to come out of the grave or to the paralytic to rise and walk.

[30]

Sons of Aaron

1. Does Calvin accept that the Romanists are in the tradition of Aaron?

After a fashion. They have a good part of the ancient Tabernacle but are missing the calves and oxen.

[31]

No Word for the Grease

1. What does Augustine say happens when the word is withdrawn from the water?

Only water remains without the word. There is no sacrament.

2. What does this do to the Romanists' anointing oil?

They have no word to show for their grease.

3. What kind of ingenious religion are they attempting to create?

They are trying to sew together patches of Judaism, Christianity, and paganism.

[32]

Duties of Deacons

1. What is Calvin's central complaint about the Romanist deacons?

That their assigned duties are nothing like what scriptural deacons did.

2. What comparison does he make to the office of apostle?

He says it is as though someone assigned "apostles" to sweep the church, catch mice, and chase away dogs.

3. Does Calvin object to the description of deacons as "sons of Levi"?

No, as long as they are kept at their true tasks.

[33]

Promise and Sacrament

1. How does Calvin amplify his teaching that to be a sacrament a ceremony must be attached to a promise?
    He says that the promise must be seen in the ceremony.

[34]

Marriage No Sacrament

1. When did the church begin treating marriage as a sacrament?
    At the time of Gregory.

2. What would happen if we allowed every scriptural comparison to become a sacrament?
    We would multiply sacraments beyond all reckoning.

3. If anyone goes along with this absurdity, what should happen to him?
    He should be sent to a mental hospital.

[35]

Great Mystery

1. What was the great mystery of Ephesians 5:28–32?
    The fact that Christ allowed a rib to be removed from Himself in order to form us.

[36]

An Inconsistency

1. What central inconsistency can the Romanists not reconcile?
    The fact the marriage act is a sacrament for them, and that copulation is, according to them, necessarily corrupt, even in marriage.

[37]

Bad Consequences

1. What bad consequences resulted from marriage becoming a sacrament?
    The church assumed jurisdiction over all aspects of marriage.

2. What did Calvin think he had succeeded in doing?
    In pulling the lion skin off the donkey.

——— CHAPTER TWENTY ———

[1]

Civil Government

1. What sort of two-fold government is man under?
   The government of the soul and the government of the body.

2. What two elements are found in the government of the body?
   The establishment of civil justice and outward morality.

3. What two errors are common with regard to this question?
   Barbarous men want to overturn civil order, and flatterers of princes want to make the civil order everything.

[2]

Different, Not Antithetical

1. As long as we live among men, what five things should we look to the magistrate to do?
   To protect the worship of God, defend sound doctrine and the position of the church, adjust our life within the society of men, to shape our social behavior to civil righteousness, to reconcile us to one another, and to promote general peace and tranquility.

2. What answer does Calvin give to those who want the perfection of the church to handle this?
   He says they stupidly imagine that such perfection can ever be found among men.

[3]

A Necessity of Life

1. What other necessities does Calvin compare civil government to?
   To bread and water, sun and air.

2. Does Calvin believe the civil magistrate is responsible to enforce the first table of the law?
   Absolutely. It prevents idolatry, sacrilege against God's name, blasphemies against His truth, and more.

3. What three components to this question of civil order does Calvin intend to treat?
   The magistrate, the laws, and the people.

[4]

Ordained by God

1. What is Calvin's first argument that the office of magistrate is ordained by God?
The fact that God uses remarkable titles for men who hold office, like "gods."

2. What enables kings to reign in justice?
Wisdom does.

3. What different kinds of rule are ordained by God?
Kingdoms, like David had; lordships, as Joseph and Daniel had; and civil rule among a free people, as Moses had.

[5]

So-Called Christian Perfection

1. How does Calvin answer those who say that Christian perfection makes civil rule moot?
By denying that they are anywhere close to perfection.

2. Where does Calvin find that God entrusts the church to the protection of the magistrate?
In 1 Timothy 2:2.

[6]

Magistrates Accountable

1. Does this mean that rulers can do as they please?
Not at all. As vicars of God, they answer to God and His word.

[7]

Monarchy No Injustice

1. Does Calvin object to the "power of one," that is, to a monarch?
Not at all. He points out that God commands us to honor the king (Prov. 24:21; 1 Pet. 2:17).

[8]

Governmental Diversity

1. Why is it difficult to say which form of government is superior?
Because circumstances vary so much.

2. What is an easy temptation in every form of government?
   The fall into tyranny.

3. That said, the fall is easiest under what form?
   It is easiest to fall from popular rule into sedition.

4. What form of government does Calvin prefer?
   A combination of aristocracy and democracy.

5. But what is a Christian's basic duty?
   To be compliant and obedient under whatever form he finds himself in.

[9]

Both Tables of the Law

1. What is central to all forms of government?
   Religion and divine worship.

2. What laws are preposterous?
   Laws which neglect what is due to God and provide only for men.

3. Why are holy kings praised in Scripture?
   Because they restored the worship of God first.

4. What is the duty of the magistrate toward the citizens?
   To protect and vindicate public innocence and provide for the common safety and peace of all.

[10]

Force and Piety

1. What question does Calvin seek to answer in this section?
   Whether magistrates can be pious men and shedders of blood at the same time.

2. What answer does he give?
   That they can be.

3. And why is this?
   Because they are not shedding blood on their own authority but in the name of God who authorized them.

4. So what should they do if they want to be approved by God?
   They should apply themselves to this ministry.

5. What defiles a magistrate's hands?
   Refusal to execute justice.

6. What is the chief gift of princes?
   Clemency.

7. At the same time, what kind of kindness must a magistrate avoid?
A soft and dissolute kindness.

[11]

Invaders

1. Why must invaders be repelled?
Because they are just robbers writ large.

[12]

Christian Magistrates

1. What is the first reason that Christian magistrates may wage war?
Because the ancient reasons for war have not changed.

2. Why is there no express declaration on this from the apostles?
Because their purpose was not the formation of a civil government.

3. What Scripture does Calvin cite on military service?
Luke 3:14.

4. Though force of arms is lawful, what place should it occupy in a magistrate's arsenal?
Everything else should be tried first.

5. What three things does Calvin defend?
Garrisons, leagues, and civil defenses.

6. How does he define them?
Garrisons are defenses along the border, leagues are treaties with neighboring countries, and civil defenses would be the things used in the art of war.

[13]

Taxation

1. What are the two lawful uses of the public treasury?
The public expenses of state office and the magnificence of official households.

2. But what is it for them to squander the resources of the people?
It is to shed the very blood of the people.

3. What is it for them to raise money not necessary for public necessity?
It is tyrannical extortion.

[14]

Sinews of the Commonwealth

1. What does Calvin treat next, after his discussion of the magistrate?
The laws, the sinews of the commonwealth.

2. What is the relationship between magistrate and law?
The law is a silent magistrate; the magistrate a living law.

3. Does Calvin believe that the law of Moses must be administered in its entirety in order for the laws of a commonwealth to be just?
No. He says the notion is perilous and seditious.

4. What common division of the law of Moses does Calvin follow?
Its division into moral, ceremonial, and judicial.

5. What trifling objection does Calvin dismiss?
The objection that there are ceremonial and judicial components to them, which he grants. He says these can still be changed without altering their moral component.

[15]

Moral Law

1. What is the center of the moral law that is obligatory for all nations and all times?
The duty to worship God and love our neighbor.

2. What was the ceremonial law?
The tutelage of the Jews that taught them the gospel in figures.

3. What was the judicial law?
Certain formulas of equity and justice.

4. What is every nation free to do?
Frame laws that are in conformity to the perpetual rule of love.

5. What ought not even be called laws?
Those that invert the law of God, such as those that honor thieves or permit sexual immorality.

[16]

Unity and Diversity

1. What must be the same for all?
Equity.

2. What is the moral law?
Nothing less than the testimony of the natural law and of conscience.

3. What is one of the places where the various laws of commonwealths differ among themselves?

In their punishments.

4. Why is Calvin fine with this?

Because the conditions of peoples vary, and different levels of severity are needed.

[17]

Christians in Court

1. How does Calvin answer those who believe Christians may not use civil courts?

By pointing out that God established them for a purpose, and that it is lawful to use them for that purpose.

2. What kind of person must not do so?

The kind who is never happy unless embroiled in some dispute or other.

3. If a Christian is in court with a brother, what must he not allow himself to be?

He must not be hateful or seized with a mad desire to harm his opponent.

4. What kind of civil courts is Calvin assuming here, pagan or Christian?

Christian civil courts.

[18]

Motives in Litigation

1. When are lawsuits permissible?

When they are rightly used and not when they come from a personal vindictiveness.

2. What must the righteous litigant be without?

He must be without bitterness.

3. How should he treat his adversary?

With the same love and good will as if the dispute was already amicably settled.

[19]

Legal Wrangles

1. Who is Calvin arguing against?

Those who say believers must stay out of court period.

2. What kind of court system is Calvin assuming here?

He calls them "Christian courts."

3. What should the aim of the godly litigant be?
   To prevent a destructive man from doing harm to society.

[20]
Public Interest

1. What does the righteous litigant maintain?
   He maintains friendliness.

2. What is he trying to increase, and what not?
   He is trying to increase the number of good men by winning his opponent, not increase the number of bad men by joining them in their malice.

[21]
Paul's Concern

1. What were Paul's two concerns in Corinthians?
   He was concerned about the intemperateness of their quarrels and that these quarrels were occurring between brothers.

[22]
Obeying the Unjust

1. To what or whom does Calvin say that honor is owed?
   He says that it is owed to the office and is not contingent upon the character of the man holding office.

[23]
Scriptural Obedience

1. What passages does Calvin cite in saying that Christians are to be obedient to their rulers?
   Romans 13:1–2; Titus 3:1; 1 Peter 2:13–14; and 1 Timothy 2:1–2.

2. Do what extent may believers be involved in politics?
   To the extent that they "have a command." In other words, to the extent that their involvement is constitutional.

[24]
Unjust Magistrates

1. Does Calvin believe that magistrates are capable of great wickedness?
   Yes, he does.

2. What does this do in the minds of men who must live under such?
   It makes them hate and curse tyrants.

[25]
A Foundational Lesson

1. What should our first reaction be when we find ourselves governed by
   a wicked magistrate?
   *We should reflect that such rulers are a judgment from God. Our
   first impulse should be repentance, not rebellion.*

[26–27]
Obedience Nonetheless

1. What does the wickedness of rulers do to our obligation to render
   obedience?
   *Nothing. Calvin cites a number of scriptural passages that tell us to
   be submissive to kings.*

2. What particular instance of such a king does Calvin use in the next
   section?
   Nebuchadnezzar.

[28]
The Royal Person

1. Whom should we serve in the civil realm?
   The one to whom the kingdom has been given by God.

2. Why are there "many princes"?
   Because of the iniquity of the land.

3. What should we then do?
   Admit this, and serve and live.

[29]
God Will Vindicate

1. What do we not examine?
   *The character of the men themselves; we consider rather the majesty
   of their office.*

2. Are we to be subject to men who are evil in character?
   Yes, even to those who are "wicked and undutiful."

3. When evil rule afflicts us, what are we to be mindful of in the first place?

Our own misdeeds that brought this judgment upon us.

[30]

Unwitting Agents

1. When God raises up deliverers for the people, what two categories do they fall in?

Some are obedient, "armed from heaven," and are doing the Lord's work. Others are tools in His hand, though their own intentions are evil.

[31]

Lesser Magistrates

1. When Calvin requires this obedience, what group is he speaking of?

Private individuals.

2. What class of men have the duty to resist the tyranny of the king?

Lesser magistrates, who have a constitutional duty to resist such encroachments.

[32]

Obedience to God

1. What is the central caveat that Calvin gives concerning obedience to the magistrate?

Obedience to man must not entail disobedience to God.

2. What denial of Daniel ties into this?

Daniel denies that he has done any wrong by disobeying the king's edict (Dan. 6:22–23).

3. What does Hosea rebuke the people for?

For obedience to ungodly edicts (Hos. 5:11).

4. And what does Peter say?

That we must obey God rather than men (Acts 5:29)

Ingram Content Group UK Ltd.
Milton Keynes UK
UKHW041046240423
420683UK00001B/17

9 781591 280866